D1713576

US SUPREME COURT LANDMARK CASES

SEPARATE BUT EQUAL
Plessy v. Ferguson

DON RAUF

Enslow Publishing
101 W. 23rd Street
Suite 240
New York, NY 10011
USA
        enslow.com

Published in 2017 by Enslow Publishing, LLC.
101 W. 23rd Street, Suite 240, New York, NY 10011

Library of Congress Cataloging-in-Publication Data

Names: Rauf, Don, author.
Title: Separate but equal : Plessy v. Ferguson / Don Rauf.
Description: New York, NY : Enslow Publishing, [2017] | Series: US supreme court landmark cases | Includes bibliographical references and index.
Identifiers: LCCN 2016026257 | ISBN 9780766084346 (library bound)
Subjects: LCSH: Plessy, Homer Adolph—Trials, litigation, etc.—Juvenile literature. | Segregation in transportation—Law and legislation—Louisiana—History—Juvenile literature. | Segregation—Law and legislation—United States—History—Juvenile literature. | United States—Race relations—History—Juvenile literature. | African Americans—Civil rights—History.
Classification: LCC KF223.P56 F575 2016 | DDC 342.7308/73—dc23 LC record available at https://lccn.loc.gov/2016026257

Printed in Malaysia

Portions of this book originally appeared in the book *Plessy v. Ferguson: Separate but Equal?* by Harvey Fireside.

Photo Credits: Cover, pp. 50, 66, 74 Library of Congress Prints and Photographs Division; p. 4 From the New York Public Library; p. 10 © State of Louisiana, Secretary of State Division of Archives, Records, and History; p. 17 New York Public Library, USA/Bridgeman Images; p. 28 © North Wind Picture Archives; p. 31 Culture Club/Hulton Archive/Getty Images; pp. 33, 58, 95 Bettmann/Getty Images; p. 40 Chautauqua County Historical Society, Westfield, NY; p. 47 Bibliotheque des Arts Decoratifs, Paris, France/Archives Charmet/Bridgeman Images; p. 90 Marion Post Wolcott/ Archive Photos/Getty Images; p. 98 © AP Images; p. 100 Robert Daemmrich Photography Inc/Corbis Historical/Getty Images.

Contents

Introduction

On June 7, 1892, Homer Adolph Plessy entered the first-class railroad car of the East Louisiana Railway in New Orleans. Although his physical destination was the town of Covington, just thirty miles (48 kilometers) north, his real destination was the Supreme Court. When he took his seat in a train car reserved for whites only, Plessy was challenging the entire system of racial segregation in the United States that had arisen after the Civil War.

He hoped this act would lead to legal actions that would eventually be argued in the country's highest court. He was striving to have laws established that would help blacks be treated as equals and gain the rights they deserved as US citizens.

In the years following the end of the Civil War, a wave of segregation had been sweeping across eleven southern states— Mississippi, South Carolina, North Carolina, Alabama, Louisiana,

This photo shows two African Americans leaning out the window of a segregated rail car.

Florida, Virginia, Tennessee, Georgia, Arkansas, and Texas. Rules were established to separate blacks and whites not only in railways but also in schools, restaurants, hotels, theaters, and other areas of social life.

When the case, *Plessy v. Ferguson*, did reach the Supreme Court in 1896, the results were not what Plessy and his supporters had hoped for. The US Supreme Court ruled that racially separate facilities, if equal, did not violate the Constitution. The Court said that segregation was not discrimination. It would take decades before separate-but-equal state laws were abolished.

Who was Homer Adolph Plessy? We know much more about the legal results of Homer Plessy's actions than we know about the man himself. Plessy was a twenty-nine-year-old shoemaker who lived with his wife, Louise, at 1108 North Claiborne Avenue, in the Faubourg Tremé, an integrated middle-class district in New Orleans.[1] All that was said about him in court, however, indicates that he looked no different from any of the white passengers. According to his lawyer, Plessy was seven-eighths Caucasian—he had seven white great-grandparents and only one black great-grandparent.

We know that Plessy bought a first-class ticket for the train leaving at 4:15 p.m. from the Press Street Depot. We do not know if he actually had business to conduct at his destination of Covington following the two-hour journey because shortly after he was seated, Plessy told J. J. Dowling, the conductor, that, according to Louisiana law, he was "a colored man." The conductor asked him to move to the "colored" car.

When Plessy refused the conductor's request, a private detective was summoned to arrest Plessy for breaking the law. The sequence of events—Plessy's refusal to move, the conductor's citing of the law, and the detective's quick appearance—makes historians wonder if the whole thing had been prearranged. Railroads had good reasons—including extra expense and public controversy—for doing away with the new "separate-car" law. They were required to set up a separate car even if only one black passenger appeared for a train filled with whites.

Detective Chris C. Cain took Plessy to be booked at the Fifth Precinct Station on Elysian Fields Avenue in New Orleans. From there, he was taken to the jail of the parish or county of Orleans for the night. In the morning he was taken to the recorder's court of the City of New Orleans where he was arraigned (that is, charged with a crime) for "remaining in a compartment of a coach [to which] by race he … did not belong, to wit, a compartment in said coach assigned to passengers of the white race … all against the peace and dignity of the State."[2]

After being charged, Plessy waived (gave up) his right to a hearing at that time. He was jailed overnight and released on a five hundred dollar bail bond. The legal record makes no mention of Homer Plessy's statements or behavior. We know that he refused to move from the seat for which he had bought a ticket. We also know from the record, that on the train Homer Plessy conducted himself civilly and did not use foul language. He was "respectably and cleanly dressed." He was also "not intoxicated nor affected by any noxious [infectious] disease."[3] If he had been drunk or rowdy, that, rather than his claim to African American identity, would have been reason enough to deny him a seat in first class.

Why did Plessy refuse to obey Louisiana law and move to a separate car? Was it just an impulse to demand that he stay in the nice clean first-class seat instead sitting in a train car that was known to be dirty? It might seem from the account that Homer Plessy acted on his own. Historians, however, have found that his stand had been carefully prepared beforehand and was intended to challenge state laws that discriminated against people because of their race.

CHAPTER 1

A Ticket Toward Equal Rights

After the Civil War in the United States, the southern states established state and local laws that enforced racial segregation. These were called Jim Crow laws. "Jim Crow" became a widely used derogatory term for blacks. Its origins date back to the 1830s and 1840s when the white entertainer Thomas Dartmouth Rice performed a popular song-and-dance act supposedly modeled after a slave whose name was Jim Crow. Rice put on blackface and acted like a buffoon, speaking in an exaggerated imitation of an African American.

One of these Jim Crow laws was the Separate Car Act (Act 111), a bill segregating railroad cars by race, passed by Louisiana lawmakers on July 10, 1890. The bill required separate-but-equal train car seating for blacks and whites.

Before the law passed, however, members of the Louisiana state legislature debated its purpose. At this time, eighteen black men who had been elected as state representatives led the opposition. One of them, C. F. Brown gave an impassioned speech asking his fellows

An Act

To promote the Comfort of passengers on Railway trains; requiring all Railway companies carrying passengers on their trains, in the State, to provide equal but separate accommodations for the white and colored races, by providing separate coaches or compartments so as to secure separate accommodations

ORIGINATED

IN THE

House of Representatives.

_____

Clerk of the House of Representatives.

Received in the office of the Secretary of State July 10. 1890.

L. F. Mason
Secretary of State

Received, Baton Rouge,_____

legislators why they would pass a law that would discriminate against hard-working black citizens. He argued that people should not be treated differently based on their race.[1]

Many whites in New Orleans were supportive of the law and saw it as fair to blacks and whites, and a just means for keeping the peace by keeping the races separate. An editorial in the New Orleans *Times-Democrat* did not hide its racism. It said that a white man who "would be horrified at the idea of his wife or daughter seated by the side of a burly negro in the parlor of a hotel or a restaurant cannot see her occupying a seat in a car next to a negro without the same feeling of disgust."[2]

The state legislators who supported segregation won and the law passed. A person—white or black—who did not sit in the proper car according to their race would be penalized with a twenty-five dollar fine or twenty days in jail. Railroad companies that did not provide these separate cars would also face penalties. If a white husband and his black wife came on the train, each would have to sit in separate cars. The only exception to the rule was for black women hired to care for white children.

Fighting the Separate Car Act

After the law was passed, many black citizens and sympathetic white citizens in New Orleans began to discuss how this law might be overturned. On September 1, 1891, the Citizens' Committee to Test the Constitutionality of the Separate Car Law was formed to

This is the historic Separate Car Act (Act 111) that launched civil rights leaders in Louisiana to seek out someone who could help them change the law.

organize a movement against the law. They held their first meeting in the offices of the *Crusader*, a newspaper that fought hard for equal rights for blacks.

The paper was founded by Louis A. Martinet, an African American attorney and physician in New Orleans. In the *Crusader*, Martinet first suggested a boycott of the railroads, then a legal challenge to overturn the law.

"We'll make a case, a test case, and bring it before the Federal Court on the grounds of invasion of the right of a person to travel through the State unmolested," Mr. Martinet wrote.[3] It would take a brave person—willing to undergo arrest, imprisonment, and a likely conviction in state court—to stage such a test.

The Citizens' Committee, which included some of the most important African Americans in New Orleans, planned the strategy and how to pay the legal costs. They raised almost $3,000 in three months—a considerable sum in those days.[4] By the end of the year, this group had found two white attorneys who would advise the group on the legal strategy.

To head up the legal effort, Martinet brought on the radical Republican Albion W. Tourgée (pronounced Toor-zhay) as senior counsel. The Radical Republicans believed blacks were entitled to the same political rights and opportunities as whites. They also believed that the Confederate leaders should be punished for their roles in the Civil War.

He was a nationally known lawyer who had been a Union soldier wounded in the Civil War. He became a politician in North Carolina and a leading "carpetbagger." (A carpetbagger was a northerner who moved to the South—often carrying a suitcase made of carpet—to work during the Reconstruction following the Civil War. They were often seen as opportunists who took advantage of the unstable social, financial, and political climate.)

Tourgée was also known for his novels, including *A Fool's Errand, by One of the Fools*, which covered the difficulties blacks in the South faced after the war.

Locally, the legal effort would be handled by the white lawyer James C. Walker, who strongly identified with the equal rights spirit of the post-Civil-War era, known as Radical Reconstruction.

Walker would be in charge of arguing the case in the Louisiana state courts. There, state judges were expected to rule against Homer Plessy. Tourgée would determine the issues based on the United States Constitution to challenge the Louisiana segregation law in a higher court. Tourgée would serve as chief counsel when the case was appealed—as the Citizens' Committee hoped would happen—to the United States Supreme Court.

Finding a Volunteer to Be Arrested

Plessy was not the first person to be chosen by members of the committee and the lawyers to test the law. That man was twenty-one-year-old Daniel F. Desdunes. A musician and educator, Desdunes was also the son of a prominent member of the Citizens' Committee. He, like Plessy, was a very light-skinned African American. Tourgée wanted a light-skinned African American to highlight that a law separating whites and blacks made no sense when some blacks were even considered white because of the lightness of their skin.

On the morning of February 24, 1892, a few months before Plessy's arrest, Desdunes bought a first-class ticket for a white coach on the Louisville and Nashville Railroad. He was asked by a train official to move to the "colored" coach. When he refused, three policemen arrested him.

Desdunes' case, however, did not become a historical test of the segregation law. Instead the Louisiana State Court dismissed it. Desdunes had bought a ticket for a destination outside of Louisiana. Travel between states was called interstate travel and fell under federal regulations rather than state laws. In May 1892, the Louisiana Supreme Court decided in a similar case that the Louisiana law had been wrongly applied to a railroad car entering the state. The state court said that the state law could not apply to interstate travel (between two or more states), based on the Commerce Clause of the United States Constitution.

Based on the ruling in this similar case, the Louisiana attorney general dropped the case against Desdunes. The Citizens' Committee celebrated a small step forward—"separate but equal" would not apply to seating on interstate trains. Now the group would test the law on trains traveling within the state.

About two weeks later, after a hurried consultation, the lawyers found Plessy, who was evidently a friend of Desdunes's father. This time the Citizens' Committee would arrange for Plessy to have an intrastate ticket. This trip would take place entirely in Louisiana. This time the federal Commerce Clause would not apply. The only issue the Committee wanted to test was whether an individual state could legally impose segregation. Was such a law in conflict with basic human rights guaranteed by the United States Constitution to all citizens?

The twenty-nine-year-old Plessy was willing to expose himself to arrest and a long series of trials in courts. He could expect to be found guilty of a crime for which he would be fined twenty-five dollars or imprisoned for twenty days.[5]

Free People of Color

The name Plessy (which was probably originally Plessis) was French in origin, as were the names of leading members of the support committee that supported Plessy behind the scenes—Martinet, Trevigne, and Desdunes (as well as Arthur Esteves, president; Firmin Christophe, secretary; and Paul Bonseigneur, treasurer). Louisiana was a French territory before it was purchased by the United States in 1803, so it is not surprising to find so many French names. Over time, the French settlers mixed with many people of differing cultural backgrounds, including Spanish, Portuguese, Native American, African, and others. Even after Louisiana joined the United States, it retained a more relaxed attitude toward racial differences compared to other parts of the country.

Especially in Louisiana's capital, New Orleans, informal connections between French whites and African American blacks had not been uncommon. One reason for this was the fact that the city was a seaport where white men outnumbered white women. As a result, there were many interracial marriages. Children of these marriages were known as mulattos, quadroons, and octoroons.

A mulatto is a person of mixed white and black ancestry, especially a person with one white and one black parent. A quadroon has one-quarter black ancestry (one of four grandparents is black). An octoroon is a person with one-eighth black ancestry (ancestry white except for one black great-grandparent). Many of their ancestors had been brought to North America as slaves from Africa.

In early America, the word "Creole" was used to describe people who had been born in the New World, and often had mixed ancestry.[6] The Creoles with African ancestry were known as *les gens libres de couleur* (the free people of color). Among them were writers, businessmen, lawyers, doctors, and members of other professions and trades. By the 1860s, they were responsible for the idea that blacks in New Orleans "were far more articulate, literary and cosmopolitan than blacks in most southern cities."[7]

After the Civil War, the Thirteenth Amendment to the Constitution outlawed slavery and segregation began to take hold. The Creoles were no longer sure of their place in society. They had identified with white society and had even been slave owners themselves. Now they found they were being excluded from the white upper class.

In 1865 and 1866, white southerners had regained governmental authority in their states. Defeated members of the Confederacy took out their anger on anyone with African American ancestry. They introduced so-called Black Codes, which restricted activities of African Americans. The laws also compelled them to work in a labor economy based on low wages. The codes would deny any African American access to schools, theaters, hotels, trains, and other places where there had before been fairly free social contact between the races. The Creoles had prided themselves on being more cultured than blacks who had been

INDAY AMUSEMENTS IN NEW ORLEANS—A CREOLE NIGHT AT THE FRENCH OPERA-HOUSE.—Sketched by our Special Artist, A. R. Waud.—[See First Page.]

This engraving of Creoles enjoying a night at the opera shows that people of mixed ancestry were treated very differently in Louisiana than they were in much of the South.

slaves. Creoles could converse in French while the newly freed slaves were mostly unable to read and write.

When the whites tried to set up a caste system—groups enjoying social status based only on race—Creoles and other blacks realized that the doctrine of "white supremacy" was their common enemy. The men who formed the committee to overturn the segregated railroad law of Louisiana were largely Creoles. They were legally allowed to marry a white person but could be arrested if they occupied the same railway cars.

Since the 1860s, they had been pursuing other lawsuits against businesses that refused to serve African Americans. Since Congress had passed the Civil Rights Act of 1875, however, such suits became more expensive. They now had to be taken to federal, rather than state, courts.[8] Whites did not want to share facilities with blacks, however. So these lawsuits became ever more difficult to win.

Plessy was a volunteer in one desperate last try to stop the wave of segregation laws in the South. The Creoles of New Orleans used this case to create a common cause with other African Americans. Not all could afford hotels, restaurants, and theaters, but they all depended on railroads to conduct business. Former slaves and Creoles donated money to cover the high court costs of this test case. The Citizen's Committee asked for contributions from rich and poor people to fight the segregation law.[9]

Plessy Takes a Stand for the Cause

The new law would isolate all persons of African descent in "colored only" cars. Before Plessy's case could rise to the national level, however, he had to appear in the state criminal district court. On October 28, 1892, he appeared before Judge John H. Ferguson. The fifty-seven-year-old judge was a carpetbagger, or a Northerner who had moved south after the Civil War, often to take advantage of the political and economic instability in the region. He had come to Louisiana from his native Martha's Vineyard, Massachusetts, to practice law. He was made a judge and assigned the *Plessy* case just a month after Homer Plessy's arrest.[10]

Lionel Adams, the assistant district attorney, had filed an "information," a charging document citing the law and Plessy's action breaking it. The information provides the details of the charges a person is facing. The original plan of Plessy's defense attorneys was to have him enter a plea of guilty. If the prosecutor and judge agreed, the lawyers would then appeal the state's conviction of Plessy to federal court.

This process is known as a "habeas corpus" proceeding. This is Latin for "you have the body." A person who objects to his own or another's imprisonment files a habeas corpus petition with the court. A writ of habeas corpus is a court order that directs law enforcement officials (police, sheriff, prison administrators, etc.) who have custody of a prisoner to appear in court with the prisoner to help the judge decide whether the prisoner has been lawfully imprisoned.

Congress had passed a Habeas Corpus Act in 1867. It protected former slaves by letting federal judges hear any cases involving a person "restrained of his or her liberty in violation of the Constitution."[11] That meant that African Americans could get a federal court to judge a state's action against them.

If the Citizens' Committee's approach with Plessy went as planned, a state court conviction of Plessy would be challenged in federal court. Eventually, the case would reach the United States Supreme Court to test the Louisiana segregation law and Plessy's rights under the Constitution.

Instead of the standard path to the highest court in the land, the defense attorneys decided on a shortcut to the Supreme Court. They would avoid a trial before Judge Ferguson altogether. They filed their briefs (legal papers) claiming Plessy's innocence. Then they asked the state Supreme Court for a ruling called a "writ of prohibition." This would stop the trial from going ahead. They argued that the law Homer Plessy broke was not valid under the United States Constitution. If, as expected, the state's highest court did not grant this writ, the case would be sent directly to the Supreme Court in Washington, DC.

On October 14, 1883, James C. Walker, the local attorney handling Homer Plessy's defense, filed a fourteen-point brief. He pleaded that the law in question clashed with the United States Constitution. He pointed especially to the key sections added after the Civil War: the Thirteenth and Fourteenth Amendments. The Thirteenth Amendment abolished slavery and the Fourteenth Amendment prohibited states from denying privileges to any citizen of the United States, including African Americans. Two weeks later the defense and prosecution lawyers argued the preliminary case before Judge Ferguson.

The trial before Judge Ferguson was in a rather insignificant courtroom where ordinary criminal cases were heard. The lawyers, however, chose their arguments carefully. The outcome in the New Orleans criminal court would probably be a guilty verdict. The state supreme court in Baton Rouge would most likely affirm that judgment.

Judges in several southern state courts had to answer to voters who were not in a mood to give up segregated racial laws. Federal judges, however, had lifetime appointments and could afford to be more impartial. Also state judges were sworn to uphold the laws of Louisiana (as well as the United States Constitution). A state judge upholding the law that segregated the railroads could argue that the conductor and policeman enforcing it had merely followed the state's rules in denying Homer Plessy his seat. A state judge was there to uphold existing laws, not change them.

In their arguments, the attorneys were preparing information that would be sent to the United States Supreme Court. At that highest level, it was not certain what would happen: Would the Court decide to uphold the Louisiana law or overturn it because it infringed on Homer Plessy's constitutional rights? No matter what the eventual outcome, the rules of an appeals court do not allow a plaintiff (the person who brings the lawsuit), to add entirely new arguments to those made at the original trial. Homer Plessy's counsel, therefore, had to make points that Judge Ferguson would reject. In this way, on appeal they could argue that the judge's "errors" should be corrected.

Showing How the Law Was Unconstitutional

Walker summed up his case to Judge Ferguson that the Louisiana law was illegal primarily because it established that a citizen could be discriminated against because of race:

> [D]istinction and discrimination between Citizens of the United States based on race which is obnoxious to the fundamental principles of National Citizenship, perpetuates involuntary servitude as regards Citizens of the Colored Race under the merest pretense of promoting the comfort of passengers on railway trains, and in further respect abridges the privileges and immunities of Citizens of the United States and the rights secured by the XIIIth and XIVth amendments to the Federal Constitution.[12]

In other words, Homer Plessy was saying that he should not be tried under a law that robbed him of the full rights of a United States citizen. This law denied him, by state power, his right of traveling in a "whites only" first-class railroad car. Further, he argued that the law left him with a "badge of slavery" by confining him to a segregated "colored" car. The state's excuse, "promoting the comfort of passengers," was not a good enough reason for enforcing a law that treated him (and any other African American) as a second-class citizen (a person who is systematically discriminated against within a state).

The lawyers for Homer Plessy based their argument on the Thirteenth and Fourteenth Amendments to the Constitution. The Thirteenth Amendment was adopted at the end of the Civil War, in 1865. It made the abolition (end) of slavery a part of the fundamental law. The Fourteenth Amendment was ratified in 1868. It made sure that the newly freed African Americans would enjoy full rights as United States citizens. Any of the southern states that had joined in the Confederate "rebellion" against the national government would be penalized. The Thirteenth Amendment is a brief statement ending "slavery or involuntary servitude" for all but convicted criminals. It is the first amendment in the Constitution to provide for additional laws by Congress "to enforce this article."

The Fourteenth Amendment contains a much more complicated text. It is open to greater legal controversy than the others. Recent civil rights cases have been based on this clause that forbids states from denying to "any person within [their] jurisdiction the equal protection of the laws." This meant that states had to apply their laws in the same way to all of their residents.

Walker and Tourgée, however, decided to link their case to a different clause of the Fourteenth Amendment. This one prevents states from infringing upon "the privileges or immunities of citizens of the United States." This meant that certain basic rights of citizens (never defined) were federally protected against state actions. They attacked the Louisiana law which, "under the merest pretense of promoting the comfort of passengers on railway trains," discriminated against "Citizens of the Colored Race."[13] In other words, the state law's concern for the comfort of travelers was not a good enough reason to deprive African Americans of their rights.

In Defense of State Rights

It was the district attorney's arguments, however, that won over Judge Ferguson. In the opinion of Assistant District Attorney Adams, the state simply wanted to avoid friction between white and black passengers on its trains. It attempted to do this by seating them in separate cars.

Adams argued that Louisiana had the right to maintain such a law because of guarantees under the Tenth Amendment of the United States Constitution, which established specific state rights. This amendment "reserves" (sets aside) "powers not delegated" (given) to the federal government "to the States . . . or to the people," as long as that was not specifically barred by the Constitution. The courts had never really defined this concept but summed it up as "police power." It was described in an 1885 decision of the Supreme Court as the states' right "to prescribe regulations to promote the health, peace, morals, education, and good order of the people."[14]

Laws that set the minimum drinking age, for example, were left to the states rather than the federal government.

What about the guarantee of equal treatment for whites and blacks that Homer Plessy found in the Fourteenth Amendment? The segregated railway law, Adams argued, far from discriminating against blacks, made it equally illegal for whites to take a seat in the "colored car" as it was for blacks to be in the car set aside for whites. In a memorable phrase, the law had called for "equal but separate" accommodations for blacks and whites on the state's railways. Whites would be subject to the same penalties as blacks if they did not take seats in their respective cars designated by race. In the real world, of course, all the cases testing such laws were brought by blacks seeking to enter cars that were indeed superior to their "colored" cars. There is no recorded case of a single white passenger trying to move to the car set aside for blacks.

Assistant District Attorney Adams appeared before Judge Ferguson on October 28 to discuss his brief. He emphasized the previous court decisions known as "precedents." In these decisions, federal judges had found nothing wrong with segregation in various types of public transportation. Then he focused on the specific 1890 law that had led to Homer Plessy's arrest.

Adams argued that this law was "reasonable" on grounds that today would be called racist. He claimed that white passengers had the right to be separated from the "foul odors" given off by blacks, and that the state needed to preserve the peace by keeping at a distance whites and blacks who could not stand each other.[15] He gave no facts to back up such prejudice, for example, where mixed-race cars had caused fights to break out.

Judge Ferguson's Decision and the Appeal

Did Judge Ferguson have jurisdiction, that is, the right to hear the case and rule on it? On November 18, Judge Ferguson decided he did. In order to do so, he had to find that the law segregating the state's railroads was constitutional. He first complimented Plessy's attorneys on their briefs. He said they showed "great research, learning and ability." Judge Ferguson then accepted the prosecution's arguments. Basically, he found precedents in support of Adams's case.

It was hardly a surprise or an event that attracted national attention. In New Orleans, however, the newspapers applauded Judge Ferguson. In an editorial, the *Times-Democrat* expressed the hope "that what he says will have some effect on the silly negroes who are trying to fight this law."[16] In the *Picayune*, the writer lectured blacks that "the sooner they drop their so-called 'crusade' against 'the Jim Crow Car,' and stop wasting their money in combating so well-established a principle—the right to separate the races in cars and elsewhere—the better for them."[17]

The lawyers knew that this was only an opening round of a long legal fight. Before the actual trial of Homer Plessy could take place, his lawyers immediately appealed Judge Ferguson's decision to the Louisiana Supreme Court. They had to write and submit new briefs. These arguments will be analyzed in chapters 3 and 4.

Next we will look at the history of the millions of other African Americans. The Civil War brought them their freedom, but in the South, they had to wait a long time before winning their battle for true equality under the law.

CHAPTER 2

A History of Discrimination

W hen the founding fathers of the United States signed the Declaration of Independence on July 4, 1776, the document contained these famous words: "We hold these truths to be self-evident, that all men are created equal, that they are endowed by their Creator with certain unalienable Rights, that among these are Life, Liberty and the pursuit of Happiness."[1]

Despite this proclamation, slavery was a part of American life, especially in the South where large plantations depended on a slave workforce. Although many northern states passed anti-slavery laws in the 1700s and 1800s, many whites in all the states did not see blacks as equals. The tide was slow to turn.

Most African Americans in the United States in the late 1800s—about nine out of ten—lived in the South. Their ancestors had been brought to America against their will as slaves since the middle of the seventeenth century.[2] Two hundred years later,

Here enslaved African Americans cut rice on a plantation in Louisiana.

they had become the center of an economy based on farming. The system rested on the idea that Christian masters had a natural right to employ slaves. Yet, most of the slaves adopted Christianity as their religion. This should have meant that their masters no longer had that excuse for not setting them free. They clung to white rule as part of the "natural order."

Beginning in the 1820s, the so-called abolitionists (people who wanted to abolish slavery), were concentrated in the North. They called for the immediate end of slavery. The abolitionists were led by William Lloyd Garrison, a Boston editor. They supported a literal application of the words from the Declaration of Independence that "all men are created equal" and were "endowed by their creator with certain inalienable rights."

At first, the majority of whites in the North, especially those in the working class, rejected the call for abolition as a threat to their own status. Eventually, however, they came around to supporting the idea of equal rights. By 1830, slavery had virtually ceased to exist in the North. The reaction in the South was much more violent. There slaveholding was justified as a necessary form of rule over permanently inferior beings.[3]

An End to Slavery but Not Inequality

Eventually the differing reactions of the two regions led to the Civil War. This was the bloodiest conflict in American history, in terms of dead and wounded as a percentage of the total population. Southerners had generally persuaded themselves that the slaves were grateful to their masters for taking care of them. Whites, however, were also terrified that blacks would revolt. They were bothered by a "nightmarish fear that the slaves would rise up, slay them, and overthrow the institution of slavery. It had happened in Haiti. Perhaps it would happen here."[4]

When the Civil War had ended, this fantasy seized the South: whites believed the uprising would take place on January 1, 1866. Nothing happened on that date. Whites, however, continued to expect the freed slaves to rise and to steal their property or burn it down.

Right after the Civil War ended in 1865, southern whites enacted the so-called Black Codes. They had lost the war but were determined to keep their political and social control.[5]

Congressional leaders reacted by preparing a military occupation of the South. It would be lifted only when freed slaves were treated as citizens.

In Congress after the Civil War, the programs of the Radical Reconstructionists were committed to protecting and expanding the rights of African Americans. They were at odds, however, with the policies of President Andrew Johnson, who wanted to show leniency toward the southern states so as to help unite the country again.

Although slaves were free, the idea that they needed to be treated as equals with whites was not universally accepted. Even Lincoln, who had called for the freedom of slaves, had been unsure about blacks and whites being treated as equals. On the eve of the Civil War, President Lincoln had assured a southern audience,

> I will say then, that I am not, nor ever have been, in favor of bringing about in any way the social and political equality of the white and black races; that I am not, nor ever have been, in favor of making voters or jurors of Negroes, nor of qualifying them to hold office, nor to intermarry with white people.[6]

Five years later, Lincoln had a change of heart. He was moved by the thousands of blacks who had fought for the Union army. On January 1, 1863, he signed the Emancipation Proclamation. This decreed that, finally, four million slaves "are, and henceforward shall be free."[7] The nation could not survive half slave and half free. But the president had not yet given a clear indication of the other postwar changes he would impose on the South.

Controlling and Appeasing the South

Lincoln had to act when Union forces occupied some sections of Confederate territory. In April 1862, Union forces under the command of General Benjamin Butler, had taken New Orleans.

This engraving shows Union soldiers pulling down the Louisiana state flag from the city hall during the occupation of New Orleans.

Local citizens named him "the cross-eyed beast." He was considered one of the most hated individuals in the Confederate states. He established a dictatorial government in New Orleans. He threatened protesting New Orleans' citizens with artillery fire and hung a man who tore down the American flag. Shopkeepers who denied service to Northern customers had their shops seized.

Butler also led the effort to build homes for ex-slaves and feed them. One Union general, Nathaniel Banks, came up with a program to employ the former slaves (although often for very little money) on the plantations. [8]

Butler urged "amnesty for all Louisianans who would take a simple oath of allegiance" to the federal government.[8] By August, eleven thousand of them had sworn their loyalty and were allowed to send two Representatives to Washington. By December 1863, President Lincoln offered pardons to all Confederates (except high-ranking officers) who would take an oath to support the Constitution. When one tenth of the formerly registered voters had done so, their state would be readmitted to the Union. The president also asked the Louisiana governor "whether some of the colored people may not be let in [to vote], as for instance, the very intelligent, and especially those who have fought gallantly in our ranks."[9]

Lincoln's policy was under constant attack by the Radical Republicans in Congress. They were in favor of punishing the Confederacy and former slave owners. Lincoln wanted to pay slave owners who were loyal to the Union, whereas the Radical Republicans wanted to abolish slavery but offer no compensation to any slave owners.

After Lincoln's assassination in April 1865, Lincoln's congressional opponents grew in power. Their forces swept the election of 1866. Their anger grew when Vice President Andrew Johnson succeeded to the presidency. He continued Lincoln's policy of moderation toward the South. He did not, however, show empathy for the freed slaves.

Rights for Former Slaves

In March 1867, Congress passed, over Johnson's veto, the Reconstruction Act. It divided the South into five military districts, each under a major general. New elections were to be held with African Americans participating. The newly elected state lawmakers had passed the Fourteenth Amendment. They had adopted constitutions allowing African Americans to vote and apply for readmission to the Union. In another bill passed over the president's veto, Congress established the Freedmen's Bureau. For a year, this sent hundreds of agents to

This hand-colored illustration shows the first African Americans going to the polls for the first state election during Reconstruction in the South.

help find jobs and homes for former slaves as well as poor whites in the South. It also set up schools and hospitals for them.

These acts of Congress were designed to reverse the Black Codes. Following the Civil War, so-called Johnson governments, under the control of former Confederate officers, had tried to keep the freed slaves in "a state of marked legal and social inferiority."[10] These codes included segregating public transportation by race. In 1865, Florida, for example, had forbidden any African American or mulatto to "intrude himself into any railroad car or other public vehicle set apart for the exclusive accommodation of white people."[11] Anyone convicted of violating this rule could be whipped with thirty-nine lashes. This was one of the laws reversed by the 1867 Reconstruction Act.

Tensions Between Races Escalate

It was not only legal segregation, however, that threatened the existence of freed slaves. In New Orleans, for example, local officials had stirred up a mob against African Americans who had assembled along with Radical Republicans to discuss holding a new state constitutional convention. Democrats thought this effort to be illegal. This effort to gain more rights for African Americans led to a riot that left forty-four blacks dead. The violence showed the deeply rooted hatred between many of the Confederate whites and the newly freed black citizens.

General Philip Sheridan, the resident military commander, reported to General Ulysses S. Grant that the riot of July 30, 1866, was really "an absolute massacre by the police ... It was a murder which the mayor and police of the city perpetrated without the shadow of a necessity."[12]

President Johnson blocked the Freedmen's Bureau when it tried to provide each black farmer with "forty acres and a mule." He was eager to return the land taken from Confederate officials to their former owners instead.

Under the Reconstruction Act, which was passed over Johnson's veto, southern states drew up new constitutions. They allowed 703,000 blacks and 660,000 whites to register as voters.[13] Southern whites condemned their neighbors who worked with the new governments as "scalawags" (a nickname for the white southerners who saw more advantage in backing the policies of Reconstruction than in opposing them). Many, however, were just ordinary farmers who had seen the Civil War as "a rich man's war and a poor man's fight."

For about eight years, from 1868 to 1876, the southern states were run by a group of whites and blacks. Restoring Confederate states to the Union was a difficult process. For many, the period was called Black Reconstruction, even though whites were the majority of voters. For the former white leaders, it became "the tragic era," in which northern carpetbaggers ran the show. Some of the northerners did take advantage of the situation to get rich. The amount of resulting corruption in government, however, seems to have been exaggerated.

The newcomers also included idealists, such as Homer Plessy's attorney, Albion Tourgée; Governor Adelbert Ames of Mississippi; and Governor Daniel H. Chamberlain of South Carolina. There were also the school teachers and doctors who volunteered for service in schools and hospitals of the Freedmen's Bureau.

In some histories of the South, African Americans are presented as uneducated. Selfish northern agents are shown as dominating state governments during Reconstruction. Of course, newly freed slaves could not have been formally educated at that time. They had been prevented from getting schooling by their masters. However, there were plenty of well-educated Creoles in the South, especially in Louisiana.

Some of the new African American leaders learned political skills quickly. This helped them to get support from one segment of the white population against another—such as landowners against populists. In New Orleans, blacks were able to integrate the public schools successfully until 1877, when white supremacists violently broke up the system.[14] The decade of educational peace in New Orleans was an exception, however.

Elsewhere the exclusion of black children from schools in the South was common. Ironically, many whites complained that blacks were not educated, but whites forcibly prevented them from attending decent schools.

As Union Troops Leave, More Rights Disappear

The Reconstruction era ended in early 1877. In the 1876 national election, Samuel J. Tilden, the Democratic nominee, appeared to be the winner. He received 250,000 more popular votes. The votes of South Carolina, Florida, and Louisiana, however, were challenged. The Republican, Rutherford B. Hayes, offered a deal to the electors of these three states. If they would give him their votes, instead of giving them to Tilden, Hayes would withdraw the remaining Union troops from the South when he became president. In the end, Hayes won by one electoral vote.

Without northern troops to support them, the governments of these states were not as compelled to uphold the rights of newly freed slaves. The state houses would again be taken over by the old elite, strengthening the power of white citizens, and they would become known as the Redeemers.[15] In effect, "the Republicans were abandoning the case of the Negro in exchange for peaceful possession of the Presidency."[16] Indeed, Hayes became president by the margin of one electoral vote, and questionable means. Thousands of Tilden ballots were thrown out to give Hayes a victory instead of a major defeat.[17]

The Congress that accepted this Compromise of 1877 was no longer the same body that had passed the measures to protect southern blacks, ending in the 1875 Civil Rights Act. That law was declared unconstitutional in 1883 by the Supreme Court. Congress then gave up on enforcing the Fourteenth Amendment for many decades. Not until the Civil Rights Act of 1964, did Congress finally provide equal rights in education, voting, and public accommodations.

The Rise of the Redeemers and Discrimination

The conservative white Redeemers put the brakes on advancing equal rights. They are credited with restoring "home rule" to the South. A deal between northern and southern business interests left the southern elite "free to oppress and exploit lower class whites and colored southerners."[18] The new national corporations paid low wages to both blacks in the cotton fields and whites working in the factories.

No sooner had the so-called Redeemers taken over than they set new records for corruption.[19] Southern African Americans lost the protection of the Republicans in Congress. The president and the Supreme Court justices also turned their backs on civil rights. African Americans now faced the full effects of Jim Crow laws.

Segregation laws spread across the South. The Louisiana law that segregated railroads in 1890 was neither the first nor the last in a series of such measures. African American farmers were forced into a system of sharecropping. Under this system, the landowners allowed the former slaves to farm the land but they had to give the bulk of their crops to white landlords. It also left the tenants with debts always exceeding their profits.[20]

So with equal rights for blacks swiftly eroding, Homer Plessy and the Citizens' Committee began their test case. He was one of very few at the time challenging the system of inequality that had been steadily growing, except for the few brief years of Reconstruction. The stakes in that last-ditch legal battle were very high.

CHAPTER 3

The Case for Equality

The success of Homer Plessy's case rested primarily on the shoulders of one man: Albion W. Tourgée, the senior lawyer in the case. Tourgée knew he faced almost insurmountable odds of winning the case before the Supreme Court because at least five of the nine justices had indicated that they supported "separate but equal" policies. Tourgée, however, had a history of resolve and a passion for fighting for justice. Even if he lost the case, he saw that the attention it would get might eventually further the cause of equal rights.

Tourgée was born May 2, 1868, on an Ohio farm. When he was young, he lost an eye in an accident while playing with fireworks. He attended the University of Rochester in New York and left school at twenty-two to join the New York regiment of the Union army. In his first big engagement, the Battle of Bull Run, the Union army was in hasty retreat. Tourgée was struck in the back by the wheel of a speeding gun carriage. After three days in a coma, he awoke in a Washington hospital. He was paralyzed from the waist down.

It took Tourgée a year to be able to walk on crutches. With credit for his military service, he was awarded a degree from the University of Rochester. He volunteered again, this time as a lieutenant of an Ohio company. He was wounded a second time in Perryville, by a piece of shrapnel in his hip. Soon afterward, he was captured by Confederate forces and spent four months in prison.

When he was released, he returned to Ohio to marry his high school sweetheart, Emma Kilbourne. The Civil War was still raging, so Tourgée enlisted again. He suffered a third wound at Chattanooga and resigned from the army when he was denied a promotion. He had worked in the fields of journalism and law before the war. Now, in the spring of 1864, he passed the Ohio bar exam and joined a law firm. Before long, he left to try teaching. He was later appointed principal of the Erie Academy, a private school in Pennsylvania.

In 1865, Tourgée became a carpetbagger. For him, however, business success was not enough. He set up a tree nursery near Greensboro, North Carolina. To set an example, he made sure his African American employees were paid good wages. It meant, however, that he was resented by his neighbors and he soon lost money.[1] He was spending much of his time making speeches on behalf of true equality for African Americans and attending meetings of Radical Republicans. This angered the governor, who called Mr. Tourgée one of the "fools and demagogues of the North."[2]

Tourgée was the founder of the National Citizens' Rights Association and the oldest historically black women's college, Bennett College, as well as a pioneer in civil rights.

Tourgée protested against the state government, which had closed public schools in order to block access to education for African American children. He limited his practice of law to the federal level. He joined with two friends to found the *Union Register*, a newspaper to carry his critical views. He was also elected to the state convention, which drew up a new constitution for North Carolina in 1868. He denounced speakers who had spoken about African American "inferiority." The following year, he was elected a judge of the state superior court. He became known for fining lawyers who excluded African Americans from juries or referred to them in derogatory language.

Tourgée was fearless in speaking out against Ku Klux Klan violence against African Americans. This meant, however, that he would soon himself be threatened with murder.[3] Eventually, in 1877, the public pressure against his family forced him to move back north, to Mayville, New York. Here he at last achieved national success as a writer of stories about his own experience. He also heard about the Louisiana law segregating railroads there. He wrote critical columns about it in a Chicago newspaper.

Tourgée's Fight for Plessy

Perhaps it was that connection that brought him to the attention of the New Orleans committee that had organized to overturn the law. He accepted the invitation from Martinet to become "leading counsel in the case from beginning to end," working without a fee.[4] The Chautauqua County Historical Society near his western New York home has a copy of the Tourgée papers.

These include letters, briefs on the *Plessy* case, and notes for arguments he would deliver in person before the Supreme Court.

Tourgée attacked the Louisiana segregation law with original arguments. He believed that the Civil War had dramatically changed the status of African Americans from slaves to United States citizens. Their newly won rights, he argued, should be protected by the federal government.

Particularly in the state courts, however, the judges were likely to see social life as still under local control by means of the so-called police power. Police power was reserved to the individual states. Judges generally reached back to previous cases (known as precedents) from pre-Civil War days. Instead of carving out new constitutional claims for African Americans while striking down discriminatory state laws, they maintained segregation.

Tourgée's briefs on behalf of Homer Plessy were short on precedents from federal courts. After a brief flurry of equal rights laws were passed by Congress during Reconstruction, the national mood had shifted to overcoming the bad feelings of the Civil War. The Supreme Court was caught up in that spirit and took quite a narrow ("strict constructionist") view of the Thirteenth and Fourteenth Amendments.

In 1883, the Court had dismissed a group of five cases filed by African Americans against discrimination in public facilities—restaurants, hotels, theaters, and a train—as beyond the power of Congress.[5] In its conclusion, the Court's majority decided that the Fourteenth Amendment barred discriminatory action only by states and not by private persons. The best that Tourgée could say about that decision was that the Louisiana situation had not yet been ruled on. Plessy's discrimination case was based on a state law, rather than private acts.

Jumping ahead to November 30, 1892, Tourgée turned to the Louisiana Supreme Court to stop the trial of Homer Plessy from ever taking place in Judge Ferguson's courtroom. Tourgée was seeking a "writ of prohibition" and a "writ of certiorari."

A writ of prohibition is an order from a higher court to a lower court ordering the judge and involved parties to stop litigation because the lower course does not have the right jurisdiction to handle the case. A writ of certiorari is a directive of a higher court to a lower court to send all the documents of a case to the higher court so it can review that lower court's decision.

These writs would allow the case to go forward on appeal. His brief covered eleven points in an attempt to declare the law segregating the state's passenger trains unconstitutional.

A Three-Pronged Argument

The argument attacking the Separate Car Act was divided into three major parts: the first called the law a vague and deceptive piece of legislation. The second said it gave unwarranted judicial power to train conductors in determining the race of passengers. The third said the law was opposed to the United States Constitution, especially the Fourteenth Amendment.[6]

Tourgée's first argument against The Separate Car Act (or Act No. 111 as the law was officially known) was that it contained inexact terms, such as "persons of the colored race." Homer Plessy and others "in whom color is not discernible," wrote Tourgée, might be assigned to either a white or colored coach depending on the conductor's whim. Light-skinned blacks would not be able to tell how they fit into the law's black-and-white division. Also, how could the lawmakers claim they were promoting "the comfort of passengers on railway trains," when it might make whites feel better, but blacks feel worse?

The real but hidden purpose of the law, in Tourgée's eyes, was to "perpetuate race prejudice." It, therefore, could not qualify as a good law that must apply equally to all citizens. The law even combined racial and class discrimination in that it allowed "colored nurses attending white children" to occupy the "whites only" car. Why not add colored servants and workers to those exempt from the law? Soon you would have more loopholes than law.

Secondly, Tourgée made a forceful case against putting train conductors in the role of determining the race of passengers. This was a power that should be decided in court. After all, it could lead to legal consequences, such as arrest, fines, and imprisonment. Obviously, that would make the law unworkable, unless each train carried a judge to decide on racial categories for all passengers.

Tourgée argued further that the conductor's power clashed with the basic legal idea that those affected by a criminal law have the right to appeal a judgment. If they proved an action had caused them injury, they should also be able to sue for damages in a civil suit. Apparently, the railroads had been reluctant to accept the burden and expense of setting up cars segregated by race. They also wanted to avoid costly lawsuits in case conductors sent a passenger to the wrong car. The lawmakers, in the final version of Act No. 111, had, therefore, blocked passengers from suing railroads and their officers for damages.

The state's attorney agreed that this section of the law was unconstitutional and should simply be withdrawn. A conductor who wrongly assigned a passenger to a segregated railroad car could, from now on, be sued. Of course, any such damages for discomfort of a passenger were likely to be minimal. The state's concession was meant to take the wind out of Tourgée's sails. He maintained the argument, however, saying that such suits covered only wrongful assignment of seats. They did not cover cases like Homer Plessy's, where seats may have been assigned correctly by race but still in a manner that a passenger considered insulting.

Against the Thirteenth and Fourteenth Amendments

The final part of Tourgée's brief to the Louisiana Supreme Court argued that the law failed to meet the standards set by the United States Constitution. This seems like the weakest section. There were few precedents from federal courts enforcing the Thirteenth and Fourteenth Amendments on behalf of African American rights. The brief also stated that key elements of these amendments were violated without supplying evidence to back up that claim.

For example, Tourgée several times cited an 1875 Supreme Court decision, *United States v. Cruikshank*. This case dealt with the "rights and privileges" granted to citizens in the Amendment.

The Ku Klux Klan was known for wearing coverings over their faces to protect their identities. They were an extremist group responsible for much violence against African Americans in the South.

Specifically, the Court in that case was reviewing a law passed by Congress in 1870 to enforce the Fourteenth Amendment. It would punish groups of people who plotted to deprive others of their basic rights.

In *Cruikshank*, members of a white mob were charged with violating that act by breaking up a political meeting of blacks in Louisiana. Chief Justice Morrison Waite wrote in that decision that it was not up to Congress to guarantee the right "to peaceably assemble."[7] That right, said Justice Waite, was not "granted by the Constitution [but] existed long before" its adoption.[8] Congress could deal only with rights derived from federal citizenship; it was up to the states to protect the civil rights of their citizens. Obviously, Louisiana had not protected the blacks at the meeting from being attacked by the hundred whites who broke it up. But that, said Justice Waite, did not involve state action, just the violence of private individuals.

In short, the Fourteenth Amendment was said not to apply, unless it could be shown that "the States [deny] the right" of citizens to receive "equal protection" under the laws. Tourgée was arguing the importance of Plessy's rights as a federal citizen. Plessy also happened to be a "resident of Louisiana." But the *Cruikshank* decision seemed to say that federal and state citizenship had equal weight. This left civil rights of African Americans to the states. In the South, however, the states were turning their back to violence by groups such as the Ku Klux Klan.

Why would Tourgée direct the attention of the Louisiana high court judges to a case that took such a narrow view of the Fourteenth Amendment? It makes sense if he wanted to remind these judges that in the *Cruikshank* case they had left the victims of mob violence without judicial remedy. Perhaps, he seemed to suggest, they could make amends by recognizing the rights of Homer Plessy to use his first-class ticket without "being thrown into prison for refusing to abide by the decision of a railway conductor." When he refused to move to a "colored car," he (and the justices) must have known that he was rejecting seating of poorer quality, even if it pretended to be "equal but separate."[9]

The State Court Decision

In any event, on December 19, 1892, the Supreme Court of Louisiana decided the case, known up to this point as Ex parte (in the matter of) Plessy.[10] It reduced the eleven points of Tourgée's argument to one question. Could the state law apply in light of the Fourteenth Amendment? Justice Charles E. Fenner, who wrote the decision, said that all other points had already been ruled out by prior judgments of the United States Supreme Court.

The only thing left to decide was whether the statute in question established a discriminatory distinction "between citizens of the United States," based on race. If it did that, the Louisiana Supreme Court said, the law would be "obnoxious to the fundamental principles of national citizenship." In other words, it was contrary to the rights guaranteed to all United States citizens by the Fourteenth Amendment to the Constitution.[11] The Thirteenth Amendment was not weighed in the decision because it extended "only to the subject of slavery," so it could be ruled out.

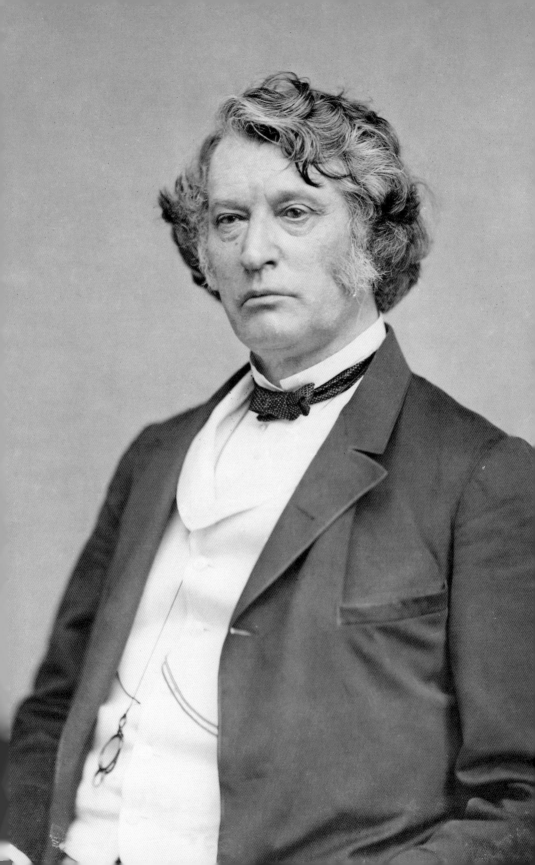

To apply the Fourteenth Amendment, Judge Fenner cited two precedents from decisions of state courts in the North dating from before ratification of the amendment. The first came from 1849. In Massachusetts, Chief Justice Lemuel Shaw of the state's Supreme Court had upheld the status of the segregated public schools of Boston against the criticism of the abolitionist Charles Sumner.

In that case, five-year-old Sarah Roberts had to walk past five elementary schools that denied her admission because she was African American. The Boston school committee would let her attend only the run-down Smith Grammar School, set aside for African Americans.[12] Fenner quoted Shaw's opinion that racial prejudice would not be caused by segregating the schoolchildren, since "This prejudice, if it exists, is not created by law and [probably] cannot be changed by law." He did not mention that the Massachusetts lawmakers had passed a law ending school segregation just six years after the *Roberts* decision.[13]

A second case was cited by Justice Fenner. In it, the Pennsylvania Supreme Court ruled in 1867 that a railroad's own rules requiring separate racially divided cars for its passengers were not really discriminatory.[14] Justice Daniel Agnew wrote that decision by deriving racial segregation from the Bible: "To assert separateness is not to declare inferiority in either. It is simply to say that, following the order of Divine Providence, human authority ought not to compel these widely-separated races to intermix."[15] In other words, God meant for blacks and whites to be kept apart.

Charles Sumner was a senator from Massachusetts, and he led the anti-slavery efforts in that state. He also worked hard to ensure equal rights for newly freed African Americans.

As for the Louisiana law of 1890, Justice Fenner found it simply to be an "exercise of the police power." Namely, the state lawmakers had expressed their view that "separation of the races in public conveyances … is in the interest of public order, peace and comfort."[16] The law was not discriminatory because it would apply equally to a white person who tried to sit in the car reserved for blacks. Justice Fenner concluded that, to force "the company of one race upon the other … would foster and intensify repulsion between them." Nowhere, however, did he cite any evidence that integrated rail travel had led to violence.

Defeat Leads to a Higher Court Appeal

The Louisiana Supreme Court's decision was a temporary defeat for Tourgée but one that he could take in stride. Under the judicial rules of the time, a plaintiff who had a negative judgment of the state courts involving a law on constitutional grounds could make a direct appeal to the United States Supreme Court. With the Louisiana court's blessing—granting a document known as a "writ of error"—that was the short cut that the *Plessy* case now took, under a new legal title, *Plessy v. Ferguson*. It would take four more years, however, before the busy Supreme Court made room on its calendar for the case.

Homer Plessy's lawyers did not move to hurry up the procedure. They thought time might be on their side. A new president could be elected in 1896. He might give new life to civil rights for African Americans. Chances for a legal victory might also be improved if new justices were appointed to the Court. Only one (Justice John

Marshall Harlan) of the nine on the Court at the time seemed sympathetic to African American plaintiffs.

This time, Tourgée called on Samuel F. Phillips, an old friend from his Reconstruction days in North Carolina. Phillips submitted a brief, in addition to one by Tourgée himself and another by his New Orleans associate, Mr. Walker. Phillips was listed as coauthor of the first brief with F. D. McKenney, another Washington attorney, who seems to have played a minor part. Phillips had been solicitor general, the chief legal counsel of the federal government. Indeed, he had thirteen years earlier argued on behalf of the five plaintiffs in the so-called Civil Rights Cases before the Supreme Court (though in a losing cause).

Now, on behalf of Homer Plessy, Phillips contended that the Louisiana law had violated his rights as a United States citizen under the Fourteenth Amendment. Specifically, he found that the expulsion of Plessy from the "whites only" car abridged his "privileges and immunities."[17] Without defining what those were, Phillips said that Homer Plessy had "sustained injury" by being treated in an insulting and humiliating fashion. The conductor's action as dictated by the state was a "taunt by law," reminiscent of the treatment of slaves before the Civil War.[18]

Phillips argued that whether or not the white and black cars were really equal did not matter because of the degradation imposed on Homer Plessy: "The white man's wooden railway benches … would be preferred to any velvet cushions in the colored car."

The briefs by Walker and Tourgée raised some basic questions not covered by the 1890 segregation law: How can it classify all railway passengers into whites and blacks, when people like

Homer Plessy, as "octoroons," have "color … not discernible in their complexion?" If the conductor exercises his powers of assigning seats, is he not assuming the authority of a judge? Why was there no "remedy for wrong," in case he made a mistake? Did Homer Plessy's seven-eighths white ancestry amount to "property," of which he was being "deprived without due process of law," in violation of the Fourteenth Amendment?

The heart of Tourgée's brief was that the Fourteenth Amendment gave an entirely new context to citizenship. National citizenship was meant to become "paramount and universal," state citizenship "expressly subordinate." Those people, including newly freed slaves, who were granted national citizenship were now guaranteed "equality of right" as well as "the free enjoyment of all public privileges." States, such as Louisiana in this case, were officially "ousted of all control over citizenship." It was a bold argument. Tourgée, however, evidently could find no judicial or legislative sources to support it.

Tourgée Argues His Case

Tourgée knew that he would have approximately thirty minutes to address the Supreme Court in person. He attempted to overpower the justices with his speech. He tried to unmask the Louisiana law as an exercise of "white class privilege," disguised by the appearance of "impartiality" (in its "equal but separate" provisions). He concluded that "no man can be hanged with a rotten rope," that is, Homer Plessy should not be convicted by an unconstitutional law.

He included references from American history in his oral argument to the Court. The Declaration of Independence, he pointed out, held that "all men are created equal," though of course it preceded the founding of the federal government. Tourgée conceded that the Constitution was drafted "to perpetuate slavery," but he argued that relations between states and their citizens had been basically changed by the Civil War.

Before the war, citizenship had been for whites only. Afterward, a new kind of citizenship offered an expanded list of rights to all—in a "classless" fashion. The federal government had formerly been charged with the "protection of slavery," by pursuing fugitive slaves and returning them to those persons who were their owners under state law (in the South). After adoption of the Fourteenth Amendment the government's role had changed, from protection of the rich to assuring the rights of the "poor, weak and despised."[19]

What would the justices of the Supreme Court make of this original argument? Would they see themselves rising to the challenge posed by Tourgée? Would they apply the Fourteenth Amendment "to secure equality of right to all against the fear of state interference?" Or would they slip back into their more accustomed role, as protectors of "wealth [and] political power,"—that is, the status quo? Before making that choice, the Court had to listen to the arguments on behalf of Judge Ferguson and the state of Louisiana.

CHAPTER 4

Louisiana's Case Against Plessy

For Louisiana, a major part of the case was to support its argument that policies of segregation were well within the powers of states rather than the federal government and upheld under the Tenth Amendment. The amendment says that any power that is not given to the federal government is given to the people or the states.

"States' rights" was a concept established under the Articles of Confederation, an agreement among all thirteen original states in 1777 that served as the first US constitution. Under these articles, the states remained independent and governed themselves. Under the Constitution that succeeded the Articles of Confederation in 1787, the federal government became the ultimate governing body, although the states still retained power and could self-govern on many matters.

John C. Calhoun, a longtime South Carolina senator remembered for his strong defense of slavery, was a strong supporter of states' rights. Starting in the 1830s, he argued that the states had powers

John C. Calhoun was a major voice in support of continued segregation and limits to African American rights.

before there was a national government. This gave them the right to "nullify," or legally ignore, federal decisions, such as those setting limits on slaveholding in the South.

After the decade of Reconstruction, described in chapter 2, most northerners wanted to end the punishment of former Confederate rebels and to let white southerners generally run their own affairs again. By the 1880s, even federal judges were caught up in this era of "forgive and forget." The movement was toward putting more control back in the hands of the states.

Homer Plessy's lawyers had an uphill job ahead of them: to have judges in the appeals courts accept their novel argument that the Fourteenth Amendment gave broad new powers to the federal government to protect African American citizens from state-sponsored harassment. In this case, the discrimination was not apparent to all. It involved merely the setting up of accommodations that claimed to be "equal but separate."

Homer Plessy's lawyers had argued that the state law clashed with various parts of the Fourteenth Amendment: Primarily, its establishment that national citizenship includes the freed slaves. They argued that freed slaves and all African Americans were American citizens who have a right to the "privileges and immunities" that all US residents should expect from their state governments—without any racial discrimination.

The attorneys for Louisiana had a comparatively easy task. They had to make the state law segregating railroads appear to be just one among many recent actions separating whites and blacks in southern states that had been approved by state and a few federal courts.

The challenge for Homer Plessy's main attorneys was complicated by the fact that his one lawyer, Albion Tourgée, was located in western New York State, and his other attorney, James Walker, was in New Orleans. The lawyers had to coordinate their strategy by the slow mail service of that time. A letter from New York to Louisiana could take about a week to arrive. They also had to work within a very limited budget.

The state of Louisiana, on the other hand, had a sizable legal staff and large sums of money for their expenses. Their courtroom representatives were Lionel Adams, the assistant district attorney in New Orleans; Milton J. Cunningham, the state attorney general; and Alexander P. Morse, a Washington, DC, lawyer. He took over the defense when the case reached the Supreme Court.

A System Favoring the State

In the first chapter, we saw that Lionel Adams did not shrink from using a racist stereotype of blacks in Judge Ferguson's courtroom. He used it to explain why white passengers needed to have their own car to avoid being offended. Next he addressed the justices of the state Supreme Court who were likely to share the same prejudice.

Louisiana's chief justice was Francis R. T. Nicholls. In 1877, he had become governor and advocated for little involvement by blacks in the political processes. In 1890, Governor Nicholls had put his signature to the railroad segregation law after it was passed by the state legislature. Justice Nicholls could now have been expected to recuse himself (withdraw from the case) because of his bias in favor of the law. He stayed, however to preside over the court that heard the case.

The first brief that the state Supreme Court justices read was from Judge John Ferguson of the Criminal Court for New Orleans, where the case originated. It argued that his criminal court was "competent to hear" the case against Homer Plessy.[1] Without going into specifics, Judge Ferguson summarized the facts of the case as he saw them: Mr. Plessy was reported to have violated Act No. 111, the railroad segregation law. The prosecution could proceed without raising "any question under the Constitution and laws of the United States."[2]

To prove that he (as well as the law) had been unbiased, Judge Ferguson claimed that he had no way of knowing whether Homer Plessy "belonged to the white race or the colored race." Was that really possible? You may recall that Detective Chris C. Cain was the officer who had arrested Plessy. In his affidavit (or sworn statement), Cain had specified that Plessy was a "passenger of the colored race" who had insisted upon staying in "a compartment to which by race he … did not belong, to wit [that] assigned to passengers of the white race."[3]

To establish so-called probable cause for a trial, Judge Ferguson would have had to have looked at Cain's statement. In the opening argument, Judge Ferguson had heard Adams, the district attorney, make clear that the law had been applied to keep white passengers from being offended by the "foul odors" of blacks—implying that Plessy was being removed at the request of whites. It is, therefore, difficult to believe Judge Ferguson's claim: that he learned Plessy's racial identity only when the actual trial started.

In his argument to the Louisiana Supreme Court, Adams supported Judge Ferguson's decision that the trial should proceed because the segregation law was constitutional on four grounds: (1) The state's "police powers" permitted the racial segregation of trains without running afoul of the Thirteenth and Fourteenth Amendments. (2) These amendments were meant mainly to protect political rights of freed slaves, such as voting, not assorted social rights. (3) The law in question did not discriminate against blacks because it had identical rules and punishment for whites who might want to sit in the "colored car." (4) State and federal courts had decided similar cases upholding segregation in schools as well as on trains and other forms of transportation.

A Biased Law

The US Supreme Court had conceded that regulation of public "health, welfare and morals" came under the authority of the various states, as part of their "police powers." It might seem that segregating railroad passengers by race would have nothing to do with health, welfare, or morals. Indeed, the Separate Car Act was labeled "an act to promote the comfort of passengers on railway trains."[4]

Plessy's lawyers had pointed out that this referred primarily to the "comfort" of white passengers, at the expense of blacks. Tourgée had highlighted this when he criticized the Louisiana law because it did not apply to "nurses attending children of the other race,"[5] meaning black nurses attending white children.

Tourgée's point was that black nurses were allowed into "whites only" cars, since that suited the makers of the Louisiana law. The nurses were considered servants, who made life easier for their white masters. Thus, the law was not really meant to promote "the general comfort" as it claimed to do.[6] It only added to the "happiness of one class"—the white elite—at the expense of blacks who were made to feel inferior.

In order to justify the Louisiana law, Judge Ferguson had to make a logical jump from the right of railroads to adopt rules to the state's right to pass them into law: "Clearly, railway companies have the right to adopt reasonable rules … for the proper conduct of their business and to designate who shall execute said regulations."[7] If private companies have this right, Judge Ferguson claimed, "[I]t follows that the legislature, the law maker, has the undoubted right to so declare in an expression of legislative will."[8]

The district attorney of course used Judge Ferguson's decision in his brief to the state supreme court. The court ruled against Homer Plessy, and the attorney general submitted its decision for review to the United States Supreme Court.

Next, the attorneys for Louisiana had to counter Tourgée's argument that such "police powers" were invalid since they violated Plessy's rights under the Thirteenth and Fourteenth Amendments.

Was Segregation a Badge of Slavery?

In the Civil Rights Cases of 1883, the US Supreme Court had found the Civil Right Act of 1875 to be unconstitutional. The 1875 Civil Rights Act said that the Thirteenth and Fourteenth Amendments were clearly intended to "remove the last vestiges of slavery" from America. The Act said that private discrimination would allow "the badges and incidents of slavery" to linger in the South. Was the seating of African Americans in a Jim Crow car a "badge of servitude," as Plessy's lawyers claimed? The Louisiana court said that Civil Rights Cases of 1883 decided that the Thirteenth and Fourteenth Amendments did not empower the Congress to legislate in matters of racial discrimination in the private sector. [9]

District Attorney Adams said that denying access to public accommodations "does not subject a person to any form of servitude, or tend to fasten upon him any badge of slavery, even though the denial be founded on the race or color of that person." [10]

In the 1883 decision, the Court made a distinction between social rights that African Americans enjoyed and the legal rights that they were now claiming under the Constitution. Supreme Court Justice Joseph Bradley wrote that, even before the Civil War, thousands of blacks who had been given their freedom were enjoying many of the rights of white citizens.

As a rule (at least in the North), blacks had been allowed into hotels or on trains, as long as their behavior was "unobjectionable." If some of them were not admitted to hotels, restaurants, places of amusement, or certain means of public transportation, they had not generally raised legal objections. Therefore, they could not now claim that discrimination by private citizens under the Thirteenth Amendment was "a badge of slavery." [11]

The Louisiana Supreme Court agreed with Adams that "the Supreme Court of the United States has clearly decided [the Thirteenth Amendment] does not refer to rights of the character here involved." [12]

As for the Fourteenth Amendment, the lawyers defending Plessy had cited three of its provisions in his favor: the clauses prohibiting states from abridging "the privileges or immunities of citizens of the United States," depriving "any person of life, liberty, or property, without due process of law," or denying anyone "the equal protection of the laws."[13]

The state's attorneys argued that all of these articles come into play only "when the States attempt by legislation to establish an inequality in respect to the enjoyment of any rights or privileges."[14] In other words, the fact that the railroad law required "equal but separate" accommodations by race prevented it from clashing with the Fourteenth Amendment. The Supreme Court decision of 1883 held that the 14th Amendment prohibited denial of equal protection by a state, but Congress could not regulate "private acts," only state laws or actions.

A Loss in the State Courts

The state Supreme Court ruled against Plessy. It had not seen any evidence denying that he had been offered "separate and equal accommodations," and turned down his appeal.[15] Of course, the judges must have known that the railroads offered no black equivalent to the first-class white car for which Plessy had bought a ticket. But apparently mere physical equality (or even superiority) of black to white accommodations was irrelevant. Tourgée's main argument was with the enforced segregation of Plessy as degrading per se. He was not concerned with the presence or absence of seat cushions in the Jim Crow car.

If Plessy had felt demeaned by the conductor's order to give up his seat in the "whites only" car, the state Supreme Court had said, that might be due to "deep-rooted prejudice in public opinion," which "is not created by law, and cannot be changed by law."[16] A segregation law by itself does "not declare inferiority in either [race] … "[17]

NEGRO EXPULSION FROM RAILWAY CAR, PHILADELPHIA.

This 1856 illustration shows an African American passenger being expelled from a white railcar.

Here the Louisiana Supreme Court seemed to shrug off segregation. It was accepted by the court as simply reflecting the way people (at least white people) felt.

The final authority for racial segregation was supposedly the Bible. The Louisiana judges refused to lay the blame for racial discrimination on people who had made laws to segregate the races. They found such laws merely "following the order of Divine Providence," that is, separating races as God had intended. It may not be surprising that southern judges held that view.

The rationale that segregation was God's will did leave at least two questions unanswered. First, it seemed to ignore the impact of the Civil War and subsequent amendments to the Constitution as indicating a new direction in history. Second, how could you tell that the current era of racial segregation was the true outcome of people's nature and God's will? In the Reconstruction era following the Civil War, integration had been the law. This had been generally accepted by the people of Louisiana. White and black children had attended public schools together in New Orleans.

The State Case Before the Supreme Court

The United States Supreme Court heard oral arguments for *Plessy v. Ferguson* on April 13, 1896. By this time the state's side was presented by Attorney General Cunningham and by Alexander P. Morse, a lawyer specializing in constitutional cases. Mr. Cunningham began his brief by saying the sudden notice from the Court had not given him time to write additional arguments. He had just reprinted the state court's decision, written by Louisiana Supreme Court Justice Charles Fenner, who "thoroughly covered the grounds presented in the case."[18]

The second brief for the state, by Morse, focused more sharply than Cunningham's on a key argument: Prior decisions by federal courts essentially did not set limits to a state's "police powers" because of rights that individuals asserted under the Fourteenth Amendment. In previous cases, such as *Barbier v. Connolly*, Morse argued, the justices had given wide latitude to a state's "regulation designed not to impose unequal or unnecessary restrictions upon any one, but to promote, with as little inconvenience as possible, the common good."[19]

Why did the state lawmakers find it necessary to segregate blacks on railroads but not on streetcars? Most of the state's blacks, Mr. Morse claimed, lived on farms, so that there was a "danger of friction from too intimate contact," presumably with white farmers they would meet on trains. In cities, however, white and black populations were more equally balanced, and they had "a more advanced civilization." On streetcars there was less "danger of friction" than on trains. (To anyone who has been on crowded city buses or subways, this argument of less "friction" here than on roomier trains makes little sense.)

The many precedents cited by Morse do not conclusively answer the question raised by Plessy's lawyers—whether or not a state could require the races to be segregated by a private company. But preceding cases do show parallel instances where states set up separate public schools for white and black children—even Congress had allowed the District of Columbia schools to do that.

In addition, federal judges had not raised major objections based on the Fourteenth Amendment when segregation had been extended to other public facilities. The trend had clearly been running for the kind of "equal but separate" law that Plessy was trying to have overturned.

A Precedent in Favor of Equal Rights

In only one of the cases Mr. Morse cited, *Strauder v. West Virginia*, had the Supreme Court been outspoken against intrusion on African American rights. This was in a ruling for a black defendant tried by an all-white jury. Justice William Strong spoke for seven of the nine justices when he said the Fourteenth Amendment had been "adopted to assure the enjoyment of all civil rights that under the law are enjoyed by white persons."[20]

In Justice Strong's opinion, the amendment had decreed that state laws "shall be the same for the black as for the white" citizens. Both were supposed to "stand equal before the laws of the states." Above all, African Americans were supposed to be protected by the amendment against "discrimination … against them by law because of their color."[21] Specifically, they were to be shielded from "legal discriminations, implying inferiority in civil society" and putting them into an inferior position to whites.

Morse's reference to the *Strauder* decision was meant to show how it was different from the situation in *Plessy*. The earlier case dealt with civic rights of the freed slaves clearly included in the citizenship defined by the Fourteenth Amendment. That was also true of the *Cruikshank* decision mentioned in the last chapter.

Distinguishing Social Rights from Civic Rights

Morse was not questioning the right of African Americans to vote or to serve on juries as protected by the federal government. But when it came to the area of social rights, Morse left the controls primarily in the hands of states under their "police powers." In his narrow reading of the Fourteenth Amendment, the only state actions that were forbidden were those that were "unreasonable." Plessy would have to show either (1) that the railroad offered him unequal "accommodations … on his proposed passage," or (2) that he was subjected to "discrimination … as a passenger on account of his color."[22]

Morse rejected these grounds: (1) Homer Plessy had not shown that he was being sent to a "colored" car that was worse than the white car. (2) Any "discrimination" applied "equally to white as to colored persons." In case the justices would question him about the poor quality of Jim Crow cars, Morse was ready to use "equal" in a very broad sense: "equal accommodations do not mean identity of accommodations." In other words, he argued that separate railroad cars—or hotels, theaters, and other "places of public amusement"—were permitted to be set up by the states as long as they were roughly equal.

The differences between white and black railroad cars at that time were obvious. The only evident similarity was that they were both headed to the same destination. Alexander Morse (who represented Louisiana Judge Ferguson), however, seemed to be counting on the likelihood that the highest judges in the land would go along with the other branches [legislative and executive] of government. Without national leadership, did African Americans have a good chance of finding a majority of the Supreme Court in sympathy with Plessy? Would the justices agree with Tourgée's argument that an African American passenger would inevitably be humiliated by being forced into a Jim Crow car? Or would they accept the common belief among white southerners that segregation would make everyone feel more comfortable, so the courts should not interfere?

The choice that the justices made in the case of *Plessy v. Ferguson* would determine the relationship between blacks and whites in the United States for decades to come.

The Supreme Court Upholds Segregation

O n May 18, 1896, the future of racial equality in the US was in the hands of eight men. One justice, David J. Brewer, had recused himself. He withdrew for undisclosed reasons, perhaps because he felt he could not be impartial in the *Plessy* case. If these justices decided for Plessy, it would be a major step toward a racially integrated society. If they decided for Ferguson and the State of Louisiana, it would create a basis for further laws allowing segregation based on race.

Tourgée thought that the absence of Justice Brewer could be a positive in their favor. In recent decisions, he had generally not spoken out on behalf of civil rights. For example, he had joined with the majority of the Court in the Civil Rights Cases in 1883. The majority held that the 1875 Civil Rights Act was unconstitutional because it prohibited acts by private citizens that discriminated against African Americans.[1]

GEORGE SHIRAS, JR.

HORACE GRAY.

STEPHEN J. FIELD.

RUFUS W. PECKHAM.

CHIEF JUSTICE FULLER.

DAVID J. BREWER.

EDWARD D. WHITE.

HENRY B. BROWN.

JOHN M. HARLAN.

JUSTICES OF THE
United States Supreme Court.

A Court Leaning Against Plessy

With one exception, none of the eight ruling justices had supported civil rights. There was Chief Justice Melville W. Fuller. He came from an old New England family but expressed sympathy for the South in the Civil War. Later, he moved to Illinois, and worked for a bank owned by his father-in-law. When he was named to the United States Supreme Court in 1888, he developed a reputation as a "defender of wealth."[2] He is known for writing opinions that found the federal income tax unconstitutional. Justice Fuller believed the Fourteenth Amendment had produced "no revolutionary change." Because of this, he felt that the law could rarely be used to defend African American victims of discrimination.

The pro-business interpretation of the Constitution was also shared by Justices Edward D. White, Horace Gray, Rufus W. Peckham, George Shiras, Stephen J. Field, Henry B. Brown, and David J. Brewer. For example, White was the one Supreme Court justice from the South. He had grown up as the son of wealthy Louisiana sugar planters. Louisiana governor Francis Nicholls, who had signed the railroad segregation law and later became the head of the state Supreme Court that ruled against Plessy, had appointed White to a vacant seat in the United States Senate.

The justices were all wealthy. Some of them, like Justice Shiras, inherited their wealth (Shiras from his family's brewery). Others made their own fortune. Justice Field had followed the Gold Rush to California. There, he became an investor in real estate. His reading of the Fourteenth Amendment was not as

This is a portrait of the justices serving during the *Plessy v. Ferguson* case.

a shield for African American civil rights. He interpreted the due process clause as protecting businesses from state and federal regulation. For Justice Field, the federal income tax was the first step toward communism. It would take the Sixteenth Amendment in 1913 to get around the Court's ruling and to make that tax constitutional.

Only One for African American Protection

John Marshall Harlan was the member of the Court who was known for his dissents, or disagreements with his colleagues. Harlan notably took a broad view of the Fourteenth Amendment as a protection for African American citizens. He did not see it as a shield for corporations against federal "trust busting." As a Kentuckian, he had actually been a slave owner. He was even a member of the racist party called the "Know Nothings."[3] But perhaps in an attempt to make up for this after joining the Supreme Court, he took a stand against anti-African-American opinions.

Justice Harlan's most famous dissent had been in the Civil Rights Cases of 1883. It took Harlan several weeks to spell out his disagreement with Justice Bradley's opinion. The opinion left the freed African Americans without protection of the courts when suffering from private wrongs to their "social rights." Justice Bradley had said that newly freed slaves no longer needed "to be the special favorite of the laws." As free people, African Americans should be treated like everybody else. They could protect their rights in court "in the ordinary modes," namely by the same means that other citizens used.[4]

Justice Harlan disagreed that the Thirteenth and Fourteenth Amendments were being stretched to make freed slaves "special favorites of the laws." Instead, he saw these parts of the Constitution designed to include African Americans as "part of the people for whose welfare and happiness government is ordained," that is, not subject to discrimination.[5]

The Court's majority told the African Americans to turn to their state governments to correct private injustices they had suffered. The justices knew full well, however, that the "white power" that had been reestablished in the South would be of little help. If the federal government were to turn its back on African Americans suffering discrimination, Justice Harlan argued, "We shall enter upon an era of constitutional law, when the rights of freedom and American citizenship cannot receive from the nation that efficient protection which heretofore was unhesitatingly accorded to slavery and the rights of the master."[6]

He was reminding his colleagues that, in the infamous *Dred Scott* decision, the Supreme Court had helped slave owners chase down fugitives who had escaped to the so-called "free states." Now it was denying federal help to those freed slaves.

An Uphill Battle

We have no transcript of the oral arguments that the attorneys exchanged before the justices on April 13, 1896. These verbal duels did not begin to be recorded until the late 1950s. We know, however, that Plessy's senior attorney, Albion Tourgée, was facing an uphill battle in fighting the Louisiana law. Recent decisions had justified other state laws setting up racially segregated facilities. The only new issue in this case was the fact that Louisiana had made it a crime for Plessy not to give up his seat in the "whites only" car of the train.

In October 1893, Tourgée had said that at least five of the justices were "against us," four of them would "probably stay that way until Gabriel blows his horn."[7] Only one of the nine—no doubt he meant Harlan—was "known to favor the view we must stand upon."[8]

A Blow for Civil Rights

On May 18, 1896, Tourgée learned that his gloomy prediction three years before had been exactly right. He must have known that Plessy's cause was lost. This became even clearer when he learned that Chief Justice Fuller had selected Justice Brown to write the opinion for the majority.

Justice Brown was the son of a wealthy northern businessman from western Massachusetts. After graduating from Yale University and studying law there and at Harvard, he had moved to Detroit, Michigan. He married the daughter of a wealthy lumber merchant and became a specialist in maritime law. During the Civil War, he refused to serve in the Union army. He hired a substitute, as the law allowed. His political activities earned him appointment to the county circuit court. Then he was named assistant United States attorney. He later became a United States district judge for eastern Michigan. His contacts with important people helped bring him to the notice of President Benjamin Harrison. Harrison appointed him to the Supreme Court in 1890.[9]

On the Court, Justice Brown could be found "in the middle." He generally wrote opinions in favor of business and property rights. Brown leaned toward the interests of railroads, which were now adjusting to the southern Jim Crow laws. But what must have been more disturbing to the attorneys for Plessy was Brown's express belief that "respect for the law [is] inherent in the Anglo-Saxon race." [10] His biographer has also found evidence of Brown's low opinion of women, blacks, Jews, and immigrants. He believed that the holders of wealth and political power were naturally meant to rise to the top.

Justice Brown's opinion in the *Plessy* case has been called one of the worst in the Supreme Court's history. To be fair, seven justices agreed with Brown. The decision did reflect the climate of the country at that time. The country seemed to be trying to forget the racial issues that had been brought to a head by the Civil War. It sought to get over the decade of Radical Reconstruction with its attempt to grant blacks equal civil rights. Southern whites had been given political control of the region since the "compromise of 1877." The decision pretended that it merely upheld facilities that are "separate but equal."

The Court's Decision

Rather than interpret all sections of this lengthy and complicated decision, we might point out the highlights:

1. Why the Thirteenth Amendment did not apply to the case.
2. How the Fourteenth Amendment might apply to a law requiring segregation.

3. What could be learned from precedents (prior judgments) in the area.

4. How a state's "police power" could extend to a law segregating railroad cars.

5. Whether or not laws could bring about racial integration.

Why Did the Thirteenth Amendment Not Apply to the Case?

Justice Brown rejected Plessy's argument that by forcing him into a segregated Jim Crow car, the state of Louisiana was pinning on him a "badge of servitude," in violation of the Thirteenth Amendment. He said, that the law "does not conflict with the Thirteenth Amendment … is too clear for argument."[11] The Louisiana law did indeed make racial "distinctions," but they did not amount to "discrimination."

The Louisiana law, said Brown, merely stated the obvious: Whites and blacks were different. That, by itself, was not the same as discrimination, or treating blacks in some legally inferior way to whites. Simply separating the two races did not amount to forcing African Americans back into slavery.

We see from this comment that Brown is taking a narrow or "strict constructionist" view of the Thirteenth Amendment: it simply forbids slavery, owning another person as property. Tourgée had argued that the amendment intended to give former slaves civil and political rights, so that the newly-freed slave would not have to "demean himself submissively" any longer to his former masters.[12]

That broad sense of the amendment was inappropriate, said Brown, citing the court's opinion in the Civil Rights Cases, where Justice Bradley had written, "It would be running the slavery argument into the ground to make it apply to every act of discrimination ... "[13] What Justice Brown did here was to blur Plessy's situation, which was the result of state law, since the earlier case had dealt only with discrimination practiced by private persons.

How Did the Fourteenth Amendment Not Apply to the States?

Justice Brown then turned to the Fourteenth Amendment, whose purpose "was undoubtedly to enforce the absolute equality of the two races before the law, but in the nature of things it could not have been intended to abolish distinctions based upon color, or to enforce social, as distinguished from political equality, or a commingling of the two races upon terms unsatisfactory to either."[14]

He is saying that this amendment, too, must be read narrowly. It implied legal equality in such things as voting and jury service, but not necessarily what might be considered fair social treatment. Critics have pointed out that judges like Brown who talk about "the nature of things" are indulging their own bias and making that sound inevitable, as part of so-called natural law. A more persuasive alternative would have been for Brown to look at the intent of the men who wrote and ratified the amendment in Congress. There were also others who followed it with civil rights laws that clearly did extend its prohibition to acts of social discrimination.

Then, how did Brown know that non-segregated railroad cars would be "unsatisfactory to either" race? Plessy was speaking for great numbers of African American citizens for whom enforced segregation was highly "unsatisfactory."

If that were the case, Justice Brown said, and "the colored race" felt the law had stamped it "with a badge of inferiority ... it is not by reason of anything found in the act, but solely because the colored race chooses to put that construction upon it." In other words, discrimination was not in the law but in the mind of African Americans forced to sit in the Jim Crow cars. The law, after all, had taken pains to equally punish Plessy for sitting in the "whites only" car and the (hypothetical) white passenger who would insist on going to the black car. For the Fourteenth Amendment's guarantee of "equal protection of the laws," Justice Brown offered African Americans the myth that putting them behind partitions on trains or in schools was offering them fair treatment.

What Could Be Learned From Prior Judgments in the Area?

Justice Brown used many state court decisions as his guideposts. He picked many of the pro-segregation judgments from the time prior to 1868 when the Fourteenth Amendment was ratified. We have already referred to two of them when we looked at the rationale for the Louisiana Supreme Court's decision in Plessy. Those cases were *Roberts v. City of Boston* (1849) and *West Chester and Philadelphia Railroad Company v. Miles* (1867). Brown's excuse for reaching back to those earlier days was that Massachusetts and Pennsylvania had language in their state constitutions that was similar to that later used in the Fourteenth Amendment to the federal Constitution.

The *Roberts* case dealt with public schools, so it was not really relevant to transportation. The *West Chester* case concerned segregation imposed by a private railway, not the state. At the federal level, Justice Brown cited "the acts of Congress requiring separate schools for colored children in the District of Columbia." However, Congress had not really required such schools—just left their racial composition to local choice.

"Much nearer and, indeed, almost directly in point," he brought up the Court's opinion in *Louisville, New Orleans and Texas Railway Company v. Mississippi*, which had been decided in 1890.[15] This case seemed to reverse *Hall v. DeCuir*, the 1877 decision in which an African American woman won damages in state court for being made to leave her first-class cabin in a boat. All of this occurred despite the 1869 law that forbade "discrimination on account of race or color" in Louisiana. The Supreme Court had voided DeCuir's one thousand dollar award. It stated that the boat was on an interstate trip and in that type of travel, laws had to come from Congress under the Constitution.

The situation was essentially similar in the *Mississippi* case. An 1888 law required segregated cars but the railway had not provided them. It was, therefore, found guilty and fined by the state. The train, like DeCuir's boat, was engaged in interstate travel. The Court's majority, however, joined in a decision that reached a different conclusion.

The justices upheld the Mississippi law on the grounds that it would be applied only in intrastate, and not interstate travel. Two dissenters—Justices Harlan and Brewer—had said they were "unable to perceive" how the Louisiana law was struck down for regulating interstate travel while the Mississippi law, though using similar language, could be upheld. A key part of that decision, however, had no ruling on whether black passengers in Mississippi could be forced into separate cars or given the choice of occupying the white car instead. Justice Brown's reference to the case implied that it pointed the way to a ruling against Homer Plessy. His case, however, raised a completely new issue: the rights of African Americans under the Fourteenth Amendment.

How Could a State's Police Power Extend to a Law Segregating Railroad Cars?

The precedents did not provide Justice Brown with a conclusive answer to the claim by Homer Plessy. So, Brown turned to the so-called "police powers" of states to judge the Louisiana law. "So far, then, as a conflict with the Fourteenth Amendment is concerned," wrote Brown, "the case reduces itself to the question whether the statute of Louisiana is a reasonable regulation, and with respect to this there must necessarily be a large discretion on the part of the legislature."[16] In other words, there should be a bias on the Court's part in favor of what southern lawmakers in 1890 had decided—that is, Louisiana's racial segregation of railroad travel.

Were there any limits to the kind of regulations made by the lawmakers? Justice Brown took the broadest possible view of its powers: "In determining the question of reasonableness it is at liberty to act with reference to the established usages, customs and traditions of the people, and with a view to the promotion of their comfort, and the preservation of the public peace and good order."[17]

That standard left Plessy without recourse. Louisiana could claim that it was just following the growing number of states now enforcing Jim Crow laws. Never mind that at the time a number of states still kept their public transportation systems integrated. How, however, could Brown talk of "established usages" when seven of the eight states that had adopted segregated travel laws had passed them less than nine years before?[18]

Clearly, Justice Brown was giving the benefit of any doubt on constitutional questions in the case to Louisiana. Within the state, the last word was reserved for the white citizens who had taken back political control in 1877, at the end of Reconstruction. It was their "comfort," not that of the state's black population, that was enough to override Plessy's claims under the Fourteenth Amendment. It was also their definition of "public peace and good order" that prevailed. The state had not shown, however, that allowing blacks and whites to occupy adjacent seats on railroads had ever caused any disorder.

Could Laws Bring About Racial Integration?

Finally, Justice Brown rejected Plessy's plea that federal law be used to protect his rights against the racist regulations of his state government. In the sociological wisdom of the time, "state-ways" had to follow "folk-ways." If the African Americans were intent on achieving "social equality," Brown said, "[I]t must be the result of natural affinities, a mutual appreciation of each other's merits and a voluntary consent of individuals." Thus, Plessy and other blacks should turn not to their lawmakers or judges to free them from discrimination but to their white neighbors and government officials.

But what if those whites were now under the spell of racism, spread by the Ku Klux Klan and other white supremacist groups? Too bad for the blacks, Justice Brown implied: "Legislation is powerless to eradicate racial instincts or to abolish distinctions based on physical differences." Finally, "If one race be inferior to the other socially, the Constitution of the United States cannot put them on the same plane."[19]

Given this outlook, there had been no major social change brought about either by the Civil War or by the postwar amendments and laws. The Black Codes from slave days essentially reappeared as Jim Crow laws. To Plessy's request for justice from the land's highest court, Justice Brown gave a blunt denial and the advice to wait patiently for society to change.

A Dissenting Voice

The only justice to disagree with the majority of the Court was John Marshall Harlan. He basically accepted Plessy's arguments: the Louisiana segregation law did fasten "a badge of servitude" on African American citizens in violation of the Thirteenth Amendment. It also denied them basic United States citizenship, with its "privileges and immunities," "equal protection of the laws," and "due process of law" guaranteed by the Fourteenth Amendment.

Harlan found Brown's opinion a disaster, on a par with the *Dred Scott* case. Dred Scott had been denied citizenship as a descendant of "Africans who were imported into this country." The Plessy decision set up whites as the "dominant race … which assumes to regulate the enjoyment of civil rights, common to all citizens, upon the basis of race."[20]

Justice Harlan said that in the area of constitutional rights there could not be a "superior, dominant, ruling class of citizens. There is no caste here. Our constitution is color-blind, and neither knows nor tolerates classes among citizens."[21] In other words, the Court's approval of the Louisiana law was a slap in the face of the equality of rights granted to all citizens by the Fourteenth Amendment. Although the state was hiding behind the "equal but separate" seating policy, it was a mere "pretense" for prohibiting black passengers from sitting with whites "in the same public coach."

Far from achieving greater harmony, this law would "certainly arouse race hate" instead. What did the majority fear from integration? "Sixty millions of whites are in no danger from the presence here of eight millions of blacks."[22]

The court majority was wrong to include the law in the state's police powers as dealing with social rather than civic equality, said Justice Harlan. The right of railroad passengers was grounded in common law. All people had the right to use the public highway.

By the reasoning of the other justices, a state could just as well require "white and black jurors to be separated in the jury box by a partition."[23] Members of the two races could be forbidden "to stand or sit with each other in a political assembly" or even to walk "in common the streets of a city."[24] The precedents cited by Brown's opinion were "wholly inapplicable, because [they were] rendered prior to the adoption of the [Thirteenth, Fourteenth, and Fifteenth] amendments of the Constitution, when colored people had very few rights which the dominant race felt obliged to respect."[25] Others dated back to the era of slavery, when "race prejudice was, practically, the supreme law of the land."[26]

A New Form of Slavery?

Justice Harlan expected the recent Thirteenth and Fourteenth Amendments to have ushered in "universal civil freedom" since they "gave citizenship to all born or naturalized in the United States" and "obliterated the race line from our system of government." Instead, he feared that the *Plessy* decision would lead to "laws of like character" in other states.

The net effect would be to reintroduce slavery in a new form: "[B]y sinister legislation, to interfere with the full enjoyment of the blessings of freedom; to regulate civil rights, common to all citizens, upon the basis of race; and to place in a condition of legal inferiority a large body of American citizens."[27]

It would take nearly sixty more years before the entire Supreme Court would come around to Justice Harlan's view. Then all the justices would agree with him that, "[t]he destinies of the two races, in this country, are indissolubly linked together, and the interests of both require that the common government of all shall not permit the seeds of race hate to be planted under the sanction of law."[28]

CHAPTER 6

The Legacy of Plessy: Separate but Unequal

While Homer Plessy was clearly disappointed in the decision, he eventually paid his $25 and returned to a fairly calm life as a shoemaker in New Orleans. Tourgée was disappointed as now America was country that upheld division by race. Soon, southern states adopted separate facilities for blacks in almost all aspects of public life, including restrooms, theaters, parks, water fountains, cemeteries, transportation and schools. They were separate from white services but far from equal.

It took until May 17, 1954, for segregated public schools to come to an end when the Supreme Court handed down its unanimous opinion in *Brown v. Board of Education*. The justices found that "separate but equal" does not work—segregation by its nature leads to inequality.

This image shows a segregated movie theater that is clearly labeled for colored people. Typically, amenities, or the useful or desirable features of a building, were not the same in "colored" facilities, something *Plessy* was hoping to change.

The Immediate Reaction

Historian Otto H. Olsen found a dozen contemporary accounts of the Court's action on *Plessy*.[1] The report in a New Orleans newspaper was favorable to the "separate but equal" ruling, since without it, there would be "absolute socialism, in which the individual would be extinguished in the vast mass of human beings, a condition repugnant to every principle of enlightened democracy."[2]

In Rochester, New York, an old abolitionist center, the decision was found to put "the official stamp of the highest court in the country upon the miserable doctrine that several millions of American citizens are of an inferior race and unfit to mingle with citizens of other races."[3]

The publication for a black church saw *Plessy* as virtually allowing any discriminatory state law (unless it took away the rights of African Americans to vote or to serve on juries) "on the ground that race conflict will arise, if the prejudices of large numbers of the white race are thwarted."[4]

A Setback for Civil Rights

Generally, the *Plessy* decision at the time was regarded as just another judicial shrug at the growing incidence of racial discrimination in the South since 1877. Thirty years after the Civil War, the country wanted to put that conflict behind it. In the process, the issue of civil rights for African Americans took a backseat. Economic growth was the national preoccupation.

The Louisiana law the Court majority had found within the bounds of the Fourteenth Amendment required "equal but separate accommodations for the white and colored races."[5] In Justice Brown's opinion, that phrase became "separate but equal," and so it has become known in our day. We know that the separate cars were far from equal in quality, but that point was not central either to Plessy's suit or to Justice Brown's opinion. The fiction of equality, however, was used by southern states to excuse segregated facilities until the 1930s.

Segregation Spreads

The Louisiana segregation law of 1890 followed on the heels of similar acts in Tennessee (1881), Florida (1887),

Mississippi (1888), and Texas (1889). In 1891, railway travel was segregated in Alabama, Kentucky, Arizona and Georgia.[6] In the wake of the *Plessy* decision, South Carolina (1898), North Carolina (1899), Virginia (1900), Maryland (1904), and Oklahoma (1907) were added to the list of Jim Crow states. Segregated transportation had been known in the South long before *Plessy*, but the Supreme Court decision now put the federal government's authority behind state laws that made it a crime to sit in cars or compartments outside of those reserved for one's "race."

The previous legal difference between the states' power to control intrastate travel and the federal government's exclusive right to govern interstate travel complicated the picture. An African American passenger who took a train from Philadelphia to Indiana could not be forced to change to segregated cars when the train crossed Maryland and Kentucky. These were states with Jim Crow laws. That would have been an "unwarranted interference with interstate commerce."[7]

As a consequence of *Plessy*, however, the Tennessee Supreme Court in 1898 said that even interstate passengers could be required to occupy separate cars. The legal distinctions were becoming blurred, as the Jim Crow barriers stretched across the region.

Punishments for Breaking Segregations Laws

The *Plessy* decision made it appear reasonable for states to punish citizens of different races who engaged in public activities, such as traveling, schooling, or enjoying entertainment together. There were at least four absurd premises behind that legal conclusion.

First, as the light skin of Plessy showed, race was not a scientific concept, since human skin color comes in a rainbow of shades rather than just black and white. Racist legislators tried to avoid any ambiguity about race by defining it in terms of ancestry. Until the 1980s, Louisiana classified those with 1/32 or more of their lineage non-white as black. How many of us could prove the racial identity of each great-great-great-grandparent?

The second flaw in segregation laws was that they claimed to punish "racial mixing" no matter whether it was done by whites or blacks. Everyone knew, however, that segregation was directed at blacks, not whites.

The facilities for African Americans received much less than their share of public funding. By 1916, for example, southern states spent an average of $2.89 educating each black child, compared to $10.32 for each white one.[8] The Jim Crow cars being used on trains throughout the South had no carpeting, heating or cooling, or clean toilets.[9]

The third evident contradiction in a state law segregating railway travel is that other forms of transportation continued to accommodate both white and black passengers. For example, in New Orleans there was a brief attempt after the Civil War to reserve streetcars for whites. Black protesters blocked the tracks and conducted "sit-ins" on the white cars in the spring of 1867 until the Union commanders revoked the segregation order.[10]

Though steamboats were segregated at the end of Reconstruction, the New Orleans streetcars remained open to all regardless of race. Later, buses throughout the South accepted white passengers first, leaving seats at the rear—if there were any— for blacks. When plane travel became common, a few airlines tried to exclude or segregate black passengers, but then common seating became generally accepted.

Fourth, as the Supreme Court permitted segregation in the social arena, it claimed that civil rights of African Americans would have full constitutional protection. It soon became apparent that an African American would not be given respect as a voter or jury member while treated publicly as a social outcast.

Following the *Plessy* ruling, new laws in Louisiana made it more difficult for blacks to vote. Registering to vote now required paying a poll tax and having a certain level of education—requirements that were difficult to reach for poor blacks. Rules established that those who had been voting prior to 1867 did not have to meet the requirements. This legal device was called a "grandfather clause." Whites dominated in the elections, and registered black voters in Louisiana dropped from 130,000 in 1896 to just 1,500 in 1904. African Americans had a majority in twenty-six of the state's parishes (county-like divisions) in 1896, but none by 1900.[11] Later, Louisiana joined other southern states that set up a white primary for nominations by the supposedly private Democratic party, which dominated the South. That practice was approved by the Supreme Court as late as 1935.[12]

Escaping Southern Oppression

In the early years of the twentieth century, most African Americans in the South had lost their civil rights. Without the ability to vote, they could not influence local, state, or national governments. They were also stuck in a sharecropping system that exploited their labor.

Here a man waits to sign up to vote in a segregated line in Georgia. African Americans during this transitional time are eager to have the vote.

The only way to escape the humiliation of segregation and the lack of opportunity was to join the "Great Migration" north. Between 1910 and 1930, more than a million African Americans flocked to industrial jobs and a chance to improve their lives in such cities as Chicago, Detroit, Cleveland, Philadelphia, and New York.[13]

The connection between Plessy's legal defeat in New Orleans and the northward migration thirty or more years later may seem unclear. Certainly, it was not the *Plessy* decision per se that weighed most heavily on the minds of the migrants. But in the early 1900s, Ray Stannard Baker had reported, "No other point of race contact is so much and so bitterly discussed among the Negroes as the Jim Crow Car."[14]

In 1944, Swedish sociologist Gunnar Myrdal still found that the Jim Crow car was "resented more bitterly among Negroes than most other forms of segregation."[15] Indeed, it became a point of pride for African Americans to avoid humiliation by not taking public transportation, buying their own cars instead as soon as they could afford them.

Later Advances for Equality

It took until 1938 for the National Association for the Advancement of Colored People (NAACP), founded in 1909-1910, to win a Supreme Court case in which the inequality of education could not be ignored. Lloyd Gaines was told by the University of Missouri School of Law that—like other African American applicants—he would have to study in another state. In an opinion written by Chief Justice Charles Evans Hughes, such discrimination was found to violate the "equal protection" clause of the Fourteenth Amendment. Only "a Negro resident" of Missouri was obliged to "go outside the state to obtain" his law degree.[16]

Other NAACP cases were presented by attorney Thurgood Marshall in the 1930s to show instances where the "separate but equal" formula of *Plessy* was not being followed. It was a tedious and costly case-by-case approach, which needed to be changed. By 1950, it had become clear that the time was ripe for the NAACP to attack the *Plessy* formula directly. Instead of suing to upgrade separate facilities for blacks to bring them up to the quality of those for whites, the target was now segregation itself.[17]

The class action suit *Brown v. Board of Education* that Marshall filed on behalf of Linda Brown and dozens of other plaintiffs led a unanimous Supreme Court to find that "separate educational facilities are inherently unequal."[18]

If *Plessy* had not been reversed in so many words, the opinion of Chief Justice Earl Warren made clear that its reasoning was no longer relevant in 1954.

The *Brown v. Board of Education* ruling faced a major test in 1957 when nine black high school students tried to enter a city high school in Little Rock, Arkansas, that was attended by white students. Governor Orval Faubus, an opponent of desegregation, sent the National Guard to block the students from entering. Undaunted, fifteen-year-old Elizabeth Eckford tried twice to enter. The standoff lasted weeks, and when students finally were allowed to enter, the public outcry among whites was so great that President Dwight Eisenhower sent in federal troops to protect the black students. Desegregation has progressed since then but is still an ongoing concern and process.[19]

Standing Up for Civil Rights

The Jim Crow system lasted until it was challenged by the civil rights movement in 1961. By that time, buses rather than trains had become the standard means of transportation. African Americans felt humiliated by having to sit in the back of the bus. They also resented having to enter terminals through a side door and being cooped up in a filthy Jim Crow waiting room without toilets.

In order to provoke action by the federal government, James Farmer, executive director of the Congress of Racial Equality (CORE) organized "Freedom Rides." White and black volunteers would desegregate buses and terminals by their own nonviolent actions.[20]

On May 14, 1961, one bus of Freedom Riders was set afire by a mob in Anniston, Alabama. Later that day, another group of

Being a Freedom Rider brought risks. This image shows a Freedom Rider bus that was on fire due to a fire bomb that was tossed through a window near Anniston, Alabama.

Riders was met by a gang of whites in Birmingham and beaten with lead pipes, baseball bats, and bicycle chains. Police stayed away. A third attack occurred on May 19 in Montgomery, the state capital. Finally, Attorney General Robert Kennedy sent five hundred federal marshals to guard African American demonstrators who had been joined by the Reverend Martin Luther King Jr. The scene of confrontation now shifted to Mississippi. There, hundreds of Freedom Riders were packed into jail for "inflammatory" traveling.[21]

When President John F. Kennedy interceded at last, the Interstate Commerce Commission pressed for enforcement of its rules against segregated bus terminals. To avoid federal lawsuits, most southern states took down the "whites only" signs. Those that did not were served with Justice Department injunctions, court orders to comply with the law. By the end of 1962, CORE was able to announce the virtual end of segregation in interstate travel—on buses, trains, and in airports.

An End to Segregation

It had taken seventy years to overcome Jim Crow in transportation. On January 11, 1897, nearly five years after his arrest for sitting in a first-class carriage for "whites only," Homer Plessy returned to the state criminal court in New Orleans. He pleaded guilty and paid his twenty-five dollar fine. The committee that had supported his legal challenge had spent over twenty-seven hundred dollars to pay the legal costs. The remaining $160 was distributed to local charities.[22] There were six dollars left to send a testimonial to Tourgée, Plessy's attorney who had worked so long without pay.

With segregated transportation finally fading away in 1962, the civil rights movement did not pause to celebrate. Instead, it went on to challenge the variety of "public accommodations" that remained divided by race. It also sought school integration, voting rights, jobs, and decent housing. Despite passage of the 1964 Civil Rights Act, the first such measure since Reconstruction, the achievement of true racial equality remains, even today, a task for the future.

One of the lessons of the *Plessy* case is that, contrary to the Supreme Court's opinion that it is not possible for "social prejudices [to be] overcome by legislation," the judges and lawmakers do not have to wait to act until people stop practicing discrimination on their own. In the 1890s, government officials looked the other way while the Jim Crow system was established and legalized by southern states.

Since the 1960s, Washington lawmakers and judges have been trying to make equal opportunity available to all without regard to one's skin color. The debate continues to rage about the means to that end. Should we continue affirmative action programs, or use busing to achieve integrated public schools? The goal itself,

Today it is not an unusual site to see students of mixed backgrounds and ethnicities together in a school setting. Thankfully the law has caught up with, or even helped create, societal norms.

however, has been recognized as a basic national value. To that extent, at least, Homer Plessy's judicial defeat in 1896 has been turned into a partial victory, as seen over one hundred years later.

In recent years, the term "separate but equal" has been applied in matters regarding sexual orientation rather than race. Certain state governments have proposed separate-but-equal marriage license systems for gay couples or separate-but-equal bathrooms for transgender individuals. African Americans have made many advances since the *Plessy* decision. America has had its first African American president with Barack Obama. Workplaces, schools, and communities are generally more diverse than they were fifty years ago and the concept of separate-but-equal facilities according to racial background has disappeared. No matter how the term is discussed, the *Plessy* case raised awareness of how the concept of "separate but equal" can create inequality.

Questions to Consider

1. Why were separate-but-equal policies directed toward African Americans established after the Civil War?

2. How was life in New Orleans for African Americans? Why do you think black citizens there formed such a strong opposition to the Separate Car Act?

3. Why were Plessy and his legal team arguing against a law that established a separate-but-equal policy on train cars? Why did they consider "separate but equal" to be unfair?

4. How did the Supreme Court decision in this case lead to further discrimination and the blocking of civil liberties?

5. Why did Plessy's lawyers believe that the Separate Car Act violated the Thirteenth and Fourteenth Amendments?

6. In Louisiana State District Court, Assistant District Attorney Lionel Adams defended the Separate Car Act by referring to the Tenth Amendment. How did the Tenth Amendment apply to this case?

7. Supreme Court Justice Brown said that laws separating the blacks and whites do not place a "badge of inferiority" on blacks? Do you agree?

8. Supreme Court Justice Harlan was the only judge to offer a dissenting opinion in *Plessy v. Ferguson*. What do you think was his most persuasive argument against the separation of the races?

9. How was *Brown v. Board of Education* related to *Plessy v. Ferguson*?

10. "Separate but equal" relates to race in the case of *Plessy v. Ferguson*. Other incidents in history and current times refer to the concept of "separate but equal" but not in terms of race. What are some of these incidents?

Primary Source Documents

Here is an excerpt from the Supreme Court's decision in the case of *Plessy v. Ferguson*. Justice Brown delivered the opinion of the Court.

The constitutionality of this act is attacked upon the ground that it conflicts both with the Thirteenth Amendment of the Constitution, abolishing slavery, and the Fourteenth Amendment, which prohibits certain restrictive legislation on the part of the States.

1. That it does not conflict with the Thirteenth Amendment, which abolished slavery and involuntary servitude, except as a punishment for crime, is too clear for argument. Slavery implies involuntary servitude—a state of bondage; the ownership of mankind as a chattel, or at least the control of the labor and services of one man for the benefit of another, and the absence of a legal right to the disposal of his own person, property and services. ...

   A statute which implies merely a legal distinction between the white and colored races—a distinction which is founded in the color of the two races and which must always exist so long as white men are distinguished from the other race by color— has no tendency to destroy the legal equality of the two races, or reestablish a state of involuntary servitude. Indeed, we do not understand that the Thirteenth Amendment is strenuously relied upon by the plaintiff in error in this connection.

2. By the Fourteenth Amendment, all persons born or naturalized in the United States and subject to the jurisdiction thereof are made citizens of the United States and of the State wherein they reside, and the States are forbidden from making or enforcing any law which shall abridge the privileges or immunities of citizens of the United States, or shall deprive any person of life, liberty, or property without due process of law, or deny to any person within their jurisdiction the equal protection of the laws. ...

The object of the amendment was undoubtedly to enforce the absolute equality of the two races before the law, but, in the nature of things, it could not have been intended to abolish distinctions based upon color, or to enforce social, as distinguished from political, equality, or a commingling of the two races upon terms unsatisfactory to either. Laws permitting, and even requiring, their separation in places where they are liable to be brought into contact do not necessarily imply the inferiority of either race to the other, and have been generally, if not universally, recognized as within the competency of the state legislatures in the exercise of their police power. The most common instance of this is connected with the establishment of separate schools for white and colored children, which has been held to be a valid exercise of the legislative power even by courts of States where the political rights of the colored race have been longest and most earnestly enforced. ...

We think the enforced separation of the races, as applied to the internal commerce of the State, neither abridges the privileges or immunities of the colored man, deprives him of his property without due process of law, nor denies him the equal protection of the laws within the meaning of the Fourteenth Amendment.

Chronology

1857 The Supreme Court issues a decision in the *Dred Scott* case finding that blacks are not considered United States citizens.

1861 The Civil War begins.

1863 President Abraham Lincoln issues the Emancipation Proclamation declaring "that all persons held as slaves" are now free.

January 1865 Congress passes the Thirteenth Amendment to the Constitution abolishing slavery in the United States.

April 1865 The Civil War ends.

1866 Congress passes the Fourteenth Amendment to the Constitution, guaranteeing citizenship and all its privileges to African Americans.

1869 Congress passes the Fifteenth Amendment giving black men the right to vote.

1875 Congress passes the Civil Rights Act guaranteeing African Americans equal treatment in public accommodations and public transportation.

1877 The Reconstruction following the Civil War ends and federal troops withdraw from the South.

1883 The Supreme Court decides that the Civil Rights Act is unconstitutional.

1890 The Louisiana State government passes the Separate Car Act, establishing separate train cars for whites and blacks.

1891 The Citizens' Committee to Test the Constitutionality of the Separate Car Law is formed.

June 1892 African American Homer Plessy is arrested for taking a seat in the first class white section of a train in New Orleans.

October 1892 Judge Ferguson decides if the *Plessy* case should move forward.

November 1892 Judge Ferguson rules that the Separate Car Law is constitutional.

1896 Plessy and the Citizens' Committee appeal the case to the US Supreme Court, which decides that the Separate Car Law is constitutional and validates separate-but-equal laws.

1909 The National Association for the Advancement of Colored People (NAACP) forms.

1954 The US Supreme Court decision in *Brown v. Board of Education* finds that separate-but-equal public schools for blacks and whites are unconstitutional.

Chapter Notes

Introduction

1. Thomas J. Davis, *Plessy v. Ferguson* (Westport, CT: Greenwood, 2012), p. 141.

2. *Plessy v. Ferguson*, 163 U.S. 537, (1896), "Brief for Plaintiff in Error," pp. 8–9.

3. Otto Olsen, *The Thin Disguise: Plessy v. Ferguson, A Documentary Presentation (1864–1896)* (New York, NY: Humanities Press, 1967), p. 11; Joseph Logsdon and Caryn C. Bell, "The Americanization of Black New Orleans," in Arnold R. Hirsch and Joseph Logsdon, eds., *Creole New Orleans* (Baton Rouge, LA: Louisiana State University Press, 1992), p. 257.

Chapter 1. A Ticket Toward Equal Rights

1. Amos Esty, *The Civil Rights Movement: Plessy v. Ferguson* (Greensboro, NC: Morgan Reynolds Publishing, 2012), p. 47.

2. Randall Kennedy, *Interracial Intimacies: Sex, Marriage, Identity, and Adoption* (New York, NY: Vintage Books, 2004), p. 23.

3. *Plessy v. Ferguson*, "Act No. 111," in Supreme Court Briefs.

4. Tim McNeese, *Plessy v. Ferguson* (New York, NY: Infobase, 2007), p. 60.

5. Thomas J. Davis, *Plessy v. Ferguson* (Westport, CT: Greenwood, 2012), p. 192.

6. Gregory Osborn, "Free People of Color and Creoles," New Orleans Official Guide, http://www.neworleansonline.com/neworleans/multicultural/multiculturalhistory/fpc.html

7. Catherine Savage Brosman, *Louisiana Creole Literature: A Historical Study* (Jackson, MS: University Press of Mississippi, 2013), p. 23.

8. "An Appeal," September 5, 1891. Tulane University Archives, New Orleans, LA, unpaged.

9. Keith Weldon Medley, "The Sad Story of How 'Separate but Equal' was Born," *Smithsonian*, February 1994, p. 113.

10. Stephen Labaton, "New Limits on Prisoner Appeals: Major Shift of Power," *New York Times*, April 19, 1996, p. B8.

11. "Habeas Corpus Jurisdiction in the Federal Courts," Federal Judicial Center, http://www.fjc.gov/history/home.nsf/page/jurisdiction_habeas.html

12. *Plessy* v. *Ferguson* (Supreme Court of the United States Oral Arguments, 163 U.S. 537, 1896), p. 9.

13. *Barbier* v. *Connolly*, 113 U.S. 27 (1885).

14. Austin Sarat and Lawrence Douglas, *Law as Punishment/Law as Regulation* (Palo Alto, CA: Stanford University Press, 2011), p. 34.

15. Otto Olsen, *The Thin Disguise: Plessy v. Ferguson, A Documentary Presentation (1864–1896)* (New York, NY: Humanities Press, 1967), pp. 14, 70–71.

16. Ibid.

17. Ibid.

Chapter 2. A History of Discrimination

1. The Declaration of Independence, *UShistory.org*, http://www. ushistory.org/declaration/document/

2. George M. Frederickson, *White Supremacy: A Comparative Study in American and South African History* (New York, NY: Oxford University Press, 1981), pp. 76–77.

3. Ibid., pp. 154–155.

4. John Hope Franklin, *Reconstruction after the Civil War, Third Edition* (Chicago, IL: University of Chicago Press, 2012), p. 3.

5. "Black Codes," *History*, http://www.history.com/topics/black-history/black-codes

6. "The Lincoln-Douglas Debates 4th Debate Part I," September 18, 1858, *TeachingAmericanHistory.org*, http://teachingamericanhistory.org/library/document/the-lincoln-douglas-debates-4th-debate-part-i/

7. Abraham Lincoln, "The Emancipation Proclamation," January 1, 1863, https://www.archives.gov/exhibits/featured_documents/emancipation_proclamation/

8. Franklin, p. 14.

9. Amos Esty, *The Civil Rights Movement: Plessy v. Ferguson* (Greensboro, NC: Morgan Reynolds Publishing, 2012), pp. 27-29.

10. Richard Bardolph, *The Civil Rights Record: Black Americans and the Law, 1849–1970* (New York, NY: Thomas Y. Crowell Co., 1970), p. 35.

11. Ibid., pp. 42–44.

12. James K. Hogue, *Uncivil War: Five New Orleans Street Battles and the Rise and Fall of Radical Reconstruction* (Baton Rouge, LA: LSU Press, 2011), p. 44.

13. Harvey Wish ed., *Reconstruction in the South* (New York, NY: Farrar Straus, and Giroux, 1965), p. xxiv.

14. Louis R. Harlan, "Desegregation New Orleans Public Schools During Reconstruction," *American Historical Review*, vol. 67, April 1962, pp. 663–675.

15. Dan Bryan, "They Called Themselves Redeemers: The Rise of White Supremacy," *American History USA*, February 26, 2012, https://www.americanhistoryusa.com/redeemers-rise-of-white supremacy/

16. C. Vann Woodward, *Reunion and Reaction: The Compromise of 1877 and the End of Reconstruction* (Oxford, UK: Oxford University Press, 1991), p. 8.

17. Ibid., pp. 18–19.

18. Otto Olsen, *The Thin Disguise: Plessy v. Ferguson, A Documentary Presentation (1864–1896)* (New York, NY: Humanities Press, 1967), p. 3.

19. Kenneth M. Stampp, *The Era of Reconstruction, 1865–1877* (New York, NY: Knopf, 1965), pp. 178–179.

20. Bardolph, p. 42.

Chapter 3. The Case for Equality

1. Richard N. Current, *Those Terrible Carpetbaggers* (New York, NY: Oxford University Press, 1988), pp. 52, 65.

2. Ibid., p. 63.

3. "Albion W. Tourgée," *Civil War Era NC*, http://cwnc.omeka.chass. ncsu.edu/exhibits/show/republicans-kkk/albion-w--tourgee

4. Robert Clayton Pierce, *From Wounded Knee to My Lai: Readings in Modern American History* (New York, NY: American Heritage Custom Publishing, 2000), p. 65

5. Civil Rights Cases, 109 U.S. 3 (1883).

6. Ex parte Homer A. Plessy, "Brief of Relator for Writs of Prohibition and Certiorari," November 30, 1892, http://www.louisianadigitallibrary.org/cdm/landingpage/ collection/p16313coll86

7. *United States v. Cruikshank*, 92 U.S. 542 (1875).

8. Ibid.

9. Ex parte Homer A. Plessy, "Brief of Relator", p. 2.

10. Ex parte Plessy, 45 La. Ann, 80.11 So.948 (1893).

11. Ibid., p. 949.

12. *Roberts v. City of Boston*, 5 Cushing 198 (Mass. 1850).

13. Richard Kluger, *Simple Justice: The History of Brown v. Board of Education and Black America's Struggle for Equality* (New York, NY: Random House, 1976), p. 77.

14. *West Chester and Philadelphia Railroad Company v. Miles*, 55 Pennsylvania St. 209.

15. Ibid.

16. Ex parte Plessy, 45 La. Ann, 80.11 So.948 (1893), p. 951.

17. "Brief for Plaintiff," in Phillip B. Kurland and Gerhard Casper, eds., *Landmark Briefs and Argument of the Supreme Court of the United States: Constitutional Law*, vol. 13, sec. 3., *"Plessy v. Ferguson,* 163 U.S. 537, Brief for Plaintiff and Defendant."

18. Ibid.

19. *"Plessy v. Ferguson*: Argument of A.W. Tourgée," manuscript no. 6472, Tourgée Papers, Chautauqua County Historical Society.

Chapter 4. Louisiana's Case Against Plessy

1. Ex parte Plessy, "Answer of Respondent," p. 12.

2. Ibid.

3. Ibid.

4. *Plessy v. Ferguson* (Writs of Prohibition and Certiorari).

5. *Plessy v. Ferguson* (Brief of Plaintiff in Error).

6. C. Vann Woodward, *"Plessy v. Ferguson*: The Birth of Jim Crow," *American Heritage,* April 1964, p. 101.

7. Ibid.

8. Ibid.

9. "Civil Rights Cases (1883)," *InfoPlease.com,* http://www.infoplease. com/us/supreme-court/cases/ar06.html

10. Charles A. Lofgren, *The Plessy Case: A Legal Historical Interpretation* (New York, NY: Oxford University Press, 1988), p. 46.

11. Civil Rights Cases, 109 U.S. 3. (1883).

12. Ex parte Plessy, 45 La. Ann, 80.11 So.948 (1893).

13. Constitution of the United States of America, Amendment XIV, Sec. 1.

14. "Brief for Plaintiff," in Phillip B. Kurland and Gerhard Casper, eds., *Landmark Briefs and Argument of the Supreme Court of the United States: Constitutional Law*, vol. 13, sec. 3., "*Plessy v. Ferguson*, 163 U.S. 537, Brief for Plaintiff and Defendant," p. 13.

15. Ex parte Plessy, 45 La. Ann, 80.11 So.948 (1893).

16. Ibid., citing *Roberts v. Boston*, 5 Cushing 198.

17. Ibid., citing *West Chester and Philadelphia Railroad Company v. Miles*, 55 Pennsylvania St. 209.

18. Cunningham, M. J., "Brief," in Kurkland and Gerhard, *Landmark Briefs*.

19. Morse, A. P., "Brief," in Kurkland and Gerhard, *Landmark Briefs*.

20. *Strauder v. West Virginia*, 100 U.S. 303 (1879).

21. Ibid.

22. Morse, A. P., "Brief for Defendant in Error," *Plessy v. Ferguson*.

Chapter 5. The Supreme Court Upholds Segregation

1. Civil Rights Cases, 109 U.S. 3 (1883).

2. Kermit L. Hall and James W. Ely, "Melville Weston Fuller," in *The Oxford Companion to the Supreme Court of the United States* (New York, NY: Oxford University Press, 2005), p. 372.

3. Loren P. Beth, *John Marshall Harlan: The Last Whig Justice* (Lexington, KY: University Press of Kentucky, 2015), p. 279.

4. Civil Rights Cases,109 U.S. 3 (1883).

5. Ibid.

6. Ibid.

7. Letter of A. W. Tourgée to Louis A. Martinet, October 31, 1893, in "The Tourgée Papers," Chatauqua, NY: Chatauqua County Historical Society, October 1893.

8. Ibid.

9. Clare Cushman, *Courtwatchers: Eyewitness Accounts in Supreme Court History* (Summit, PA: Rowman & Littlefield, 2011), p. 71.

10. Hall and Ely, p. 110.

11. *Plessy v. Ferguson,* 163 U.S. 537 (1896)

12. *Plessy v. Ferguson* (Brief of Plaintiff in Error).

13. *Plessy v. Ferguson,* 163 U.S. 537 (1896).

14. Ibid.

15. *Louisville, New Orleans and Texas Railway Company v. Mississippi,* 133 U.S. 587 (1890).

16. *Plessy v. Ferguson,* 163 U.S. 537 (1896).

17. Ibid.

18. Kluger, p. 80.

19. *Plessy v. Ferguson,* 163 U.S. 537 (1896).

20. Ibid.

21. Ibid.

22. Ibid.

23. Ibid.

24. Ibid.

25. Ibid.

26. Ibid.

27. Ibid.

28. Ibid.

Chapter 6. The Legacy of Plessy: Separate but Unequal

1. Otto Olsen, *The Thin Disguise: Plessy v. Ferguson, A Documentary Presentation (1864–1896)* (New York, NY: Humanities Press, 1967), pp. 123–130.

2. *Daily Picayune*, May 19, 1896.

3. *Democrat and Chronicle*, May 20, 1896.

4. *A.M.E. Church Review*, vol.12, pp. 156–162.

5. Ex parte Plessy, 45 La. Ann, 80.11 So.948 (1893).

6. Gilbert T. Stephenson, *Race Distinctions in American Law* (New York, NY: D. Appleton & Co., 1910), p. 216.

7. Ibid., p. 218.

8. Richard Kluger, *Simple Justice: The History of Brown v. Board of Education and Black America's Struggle for Equality* (New York, NY: Random House, 1976), p. 88.

9. Catherine A. Barnes, *Journey from Jim Crow: The Desegregation of Southern Transit* (New York, NY: Columbia University Press, 1983), p. 15.

10. Ibid., p. 3.

11. Ibid., p. 15.

12. *Grovey v. Townsend*, 295 U.S. 45 (1935).

13. Karl Taeuber and Alma Taeuber, *Negroes in Cities: Residential Segregation and Neighborhood Change* (Chicago, IL: Aldine, 1965), p. 3.

14. John C. Inscoe, *Writing the South Through the Self: Explorations in Southern Autobiography* (Athens, GA: University of Georgia Press, 2011), p. 100.

15. Ibid.

16. *Missouri ex rel. Gaines v. Canada*, 305 U.S. 337 (1938).

17. Mark Tushnet, *The NAACP's Legal Strategy Against Segregated Education, 1925–1950* (Chapel Hill, NC: University of North Carolina Press, 1987), p. 105.

18. *Brown vs. Board of Education*, 347 U.S. 483 (1953).

19. Esty, pp. 100-101.

20. Robert Weisbrot, *Freedom Bound: A History of America's Civil Right's Movement* (New York, NY: Penguin Books, 1991), p. 55.

21. Ibid., p. 61.

22. Charles A. Lofgren, *The Plessy Case: A Legal Historical Interpretation* (New York, NY: Oxford University Press, 1988), 208.

Glossary

abolitionists People who wanted the immediate freedom of the slaves; organizations spreading around the country since the 1830s.

arraign To call someone before a court of law to be charged.

bail A pledge of money or property to guarantee that someone accused of a crime will appear at trial; the bail may get paid to the court if the defendant fails to appear.

Black Codes Laws to control the newly freed slaves. The laws were passed by southern state governments under President Andrew Johnson. They prohibited blacks from voting, sitting on juries, and doing many other things that whites could do.

brief Written arguments about the law and facts presented by the parties to a lawsuit. Briefs are written to persuade the court to decide in favor of the party's particular position.

carpetbaggers A negative term for northerners who came to the South after the Civil War to start businesses and to encourage former slaves to vote and own land. "Carpetbaggers" was the nickname used for them because they had packed a few belongings in suitcases made from squares of carpet. They were blamed by white southerners for the political turmoil of Reconstruction.

civil suit Action in court under non-criminal law. Such lawsuits are usually to recover money, to stop someone who is causing an injury, or to decide someone's rights. Unless a party ignores a judge's order, no one is sent to jail in a civil suit.

Commerce Clause Article I, Section 8, of the Constitution, which gives Congress the right "to regulate commerce with foreign nations [and] among the several states."

common law "Judge-made law," which the United States adopted from England, where it was supposed to reflect the customary rules of the nation.

court Judge or judges who sit and listen to arguments and order people to obey the law or write decisions are called "the court."

defendant The party (or person) in a lawsuit who is being sued. The other party claims to have been wronged by the defendant. A defendant in a criminal case is the person accused of the crime.

dissent An opinion written by a judge who disagrees with the opinion of the majority of the court.

grandfather clause Southern state laws that said everyone had to take a test in order to vote unless their grandfather had voted. These clauses were designed to deny African Americans, whose grandfathers had been slaves, the right to vote.

habeas corpus Literally, "you have the body"—a court order, dating from the Middle Ages in England. It asked the king to release prisoners who were illegally detained. This right was guaranteed by Article I of the United States Constitution and enacted in an 1867 act of Congress to protect freed slaves.

Johnson governments Southern state governments set up under President Johnson's authority right after the Civil War. Since they were generally run by former Confederate officers, they enacted Black Codes, which kept freed slaves in a condition of inferiority.

jurisdiction A court can hear a case only if a law says such a case can be heard by that court. If, for example, you sued someone in your state based only on state law, a federal court would not be able to listen to your case—it does not have jurisdiction.

natural law A belief that certain laws can be derived from nature, in addition to laws passed by a legislature.

police power The power of the states recognized in the Tenth Amendment of the United States Constitution to pass and enforce laws to protect the health and safety of their citizens.

precedent All of the prior decisions on an issue that is presently before a court. The court is supposed to decide a case in a way that is consistent with decisions that have come before it.

Radical Reconstruction The policies of the abolitionists in the Republican Party in the Civil War period. They were designed to punish the South and to protect the rights of the freed slaves.

recuse Literally, "to refuse." It refers to a judge's or justice's decision to be excused from a case in which he or she has a possible bias.

Redeemers The old white ruling class in the South that returned to power in the late 1870s and restored a system that denied blacks and poor whites a share of power.

scalawags A name given to southern politicians who shared power during the Reconstruction period with carpetbaggers. Though they were blamed for economic problems, they reformed education and voting laws to give access to African Americans.

states' rights A political view that upholds the powers of the states as opposed to those of the federal government. In an extreme form, it argues that states should have veto power over acts of the central government.

strict constructionist Someone who believes in interpreting words exactly as they are written. These people read the United States Constitution to allow only the stated powers to the federal government but not those that are implied; they thus leave all other decisions to the states and believe in states' rights.

white primary A law used by southern states to deny the right to vote in primary elections to African Americans. Since the Democratic Party controlled the "Solid South" after Reconstruction, the Democratic primary vote in effect decided who won office in the general election.

writ of certiorari An order issued by the United States Supreme Court by which it announces it will review decisions by lower federal or state courts. It is the most common way for cases to be heard by the Supreme Court and usually requires the agreement of at least four of the nine justices.

writ of prohibition An unusual order issued by a higher to a lower court that commands it to drop a case over which it lacks jurisdiction.

Further Reading

Books

Cates, David and Melissa York. *Plessy v. Ferguson: Segregation and the Separate but Equal Policy (Landmark Supreme Court Cases)*. Minneapolis, MN: Abdo Publishing Company, 2012.

Esty, Amos. *The Civil Rights Movement: Plessy v. Ferguson*. Greensboro, NC: Morgan Reynolds Publishing, 2012.

Fireside, Harvey. *Separate and Unequal: Homer Plessy and the Supreme Court Decision That Legalized Racism*. New York, NY: Carol & Graf Publishers, 2004.

Hill, Lena M. *Jim Crow in America: A Historical Exploration of Literature*. Westport, CT: Greenwood, 2016.

Websites

Charters of Freedom: US Constitutional Amendments 11-27

www.archives.gov/exhibits/charters/constitution_amendments_11-27.html

This site contains the wording to the Constitution as well as all its amendments.

The National Association for the Advancement of Colored People

www.naacp.org

The NAACP exists to ensure the political, educational, social, and economic equality of rights of all persons and to eliminate race-based discrimination.

OurDocuments.gov

www.ourdocuments.gov/doc.php?doc=52

This source provides transcripts of many milestone documents in US history.

Supreme Court of the United States

www.supremecourt.gov

This site features opinions, oral arguments, and case documents from the country's highest court.

Index

H

habeas corpus, 19

Hall v. DeCuir, 83

Harlan, John Marshall, 53, 76, 77, 78, 84, 86, 87, 88

Harrison, Benjamin, 78

Hayes, Rutherford B., 36, 37

Hughes, Charles Evans, 96

I

interstate commerce, 92, 98

J

Jim Crow car, 25, 64, 65, 70, 71, 80, 82, 93, 95

Jim Crow laws, 9, 38, 79, 85, 86, 92, 97, 99

Johnson, Andrew, 30, 32, 34, 35

K

Kennedy, John F., 98

Kennedy, Robert, 98

Kilbourne, Emma, 41

King Jr., Martin Luther, 98

Ku Klux Klan, 42, 48, 86

L

Lincoln, Abraham, 30, 32

Louisiana railroad segregation law, 60, 61, 75

Louisiana Supreme Court, 14, 25, 44, 46, 49, 52, 62, 64, 67, 68, 82

Louisville and Nashville Railroad, 14

Louisville, New Orleans and Texas Railway Company v. Mississippi, 83

M

Marshall, Thurgood, 96

Martinet, Louis A., 12, 15, 42

McKenney, F. D., 53

Morse, Alexander P., 60, 67, 68, 69, 70

mulattos, 15, 34

Myrdal, Gunnar, 95

N

National Association for the Advancement of Colored People (NAACP), 96

New Orleans, 5, 6, 7, 11, 12, 15, 16, 18, 20, 25, 30, 31, 34, 36, 42, 53, 60, 61, 67, 89, 90, 93, 95, 99

Nicholls, Francis R. T., 60, 75

O

Obama, Barack, 100

octoroons, 15, 16, 54

Olson, Otto H., 90

P

Peckham, Rufus W., 75

Phillips, Samuel F., 53